A Christian Woman Book
For Better, For Worse?

Julie Reeves has been married for sixteen years and is the mother of four sons. A freelance writer, she contributed to the volume on *Creativity* in the Christian Woman series, and has also written for *Christian Woman* magazine. She lives in Hampshire, and with her husband, who is a college lecturer, has been responsible for setting up a Christian bookshop and third world craft centre.

GW00694280

Christian Woman Books

Series Editor: Gail Lawther

Other titles in preparation

For Better, For Worse?

A realistic view of problems
in Christian marriage

JULIE REEVES

First published 1986
Triangle
SPCK
Holy Trinity Church
Marylebone Road
London NW1 4DU

British Library Cataloguing in Publication Data

Reeves, Julie
    For better, for worse?: a realistic view
    of problems in Christian marriage.—
    (Christian woman books)
    1. Marriage—Religious aspects—
    Christianity
    I. Title   II. Series
    261.8′3581   BT706

    ISBN 0-281-04245-4

Phototypeset by Input Typesetting Ltd, London
Printed in Great Britain by
Hazell Watson & Viney Ltd
Member of the BPCC Group
Aylesbury, Bucks

Contents

Series Editor's Foreword

Christian women are developing a new awareness of the way our faith touches every part of our lives. Women who have always lived in a Christian environment are facing up to the important issues in the world around them. Women who have found in Christ a new direction for living are seeking to sort out the problems that are hampering their spiritual growth. And many women are rediscovering the joy in using their God-given talents, in their relationships with God and with other people, and in their spiritual lives and worship. *Christian Woman* magazine has been privileged to be part of this learning process.

As a result of this deepening awareness and commitment to Christianity, many books have been published which help women to sort out what God can do for them as women, as wives, as career people, as mothers, as single women. Most of these books however have been rooted in the American culture; this *Christian Woman* series has come into being because we believe it is important that we have books that talk our own language, and are relevant to everyday life in our own culture.

Each book in this series will deal with some aspect of living as a Christian woman in today's world. I am delighted that we have been able to be part of the blossoming of God's church in this way. We hope that the books will help you as a Christian woman to overcome problems, enrich your life and your relationships, learn more of God, think through important issues, enjoy your femininity, make wise choices, and deepen your commitment to Jesus Christ.

In these books we have invited people to share what they have learned about living as Christians. Not everyone will agree with all the ideas expressed in each book, but I know that you will find every book in the series interesting and thought-provoking.

Books change peoples lives – perhaps these books will change your life.

GAIL LAWTHER

Introduction

Not Another One!

It may seem presumptuous for a relatively inexperienced writer, who has struggled through only sixteen years of marriage, to attempt to produce a book about it. There is plenty of good literature on the subject already, so what do I hope to achieve by presenting you with yet another book on Christian marriage?

I should like the main achievement of this book to be to dispel the myth that Christians should expect marriage to be plain sailing provided they follow certain guidelines, and that they can expect to be immune from the epidemic of broken relationships. As I recently heard Selwyn Hughes say, 'In most churches people with problems are about as welcome as a pork pie in a synagogue!' and indeed that is how those with ailing marriages are often made to feel. All the examples in this book are taken from real life, and that should be sufficient to show that problems abound, even (or perhaps especially) in Christian marriages, and that many people would benefit from being more willing to admit to them.

This book is written for those whose marriage doesn't conform to any set pattern, far less the pattern laid down in the Bible, and yet who are seeking to live as Christians. It acknowledges that a good marriage has to be worked at, but that every couple is different and will not necessarily benefit from the same advice or suggestions as their neighbours. If you've ever felt like giving up or have actually given up trying, or if you wish you'd never started in the first place, this book is for you. So if you have a difficult marriage, read it for encouragement, and if you have a good one, read it for a greater understanding of other people's problems and for an idea of how to cope if the going gets rough.

I should like to dedicate this book to my husband, John, who has made a vital contribution to it in more ways than one. His love and encouragement and belief in me have enabled me to keep writing, but without his imperfections (coupled with mine) many of the problems described here would not have occurred!

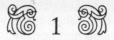

'I Know My Place' – or Do I?

Once upon a time, every one had a place: they may not have liked it but at least they knew what it was. Life was hard for those who had to work for a living, and few of us would want to return to those conditions, yet somehow, with all our labour-saving devices, many of us live at a terrific rate and have little time to devote to our families. Not only are the divorce and separation statistics frighteningly high, but so is the incidence of mental illness and suicide – not to mention the number of women on tranquillisers. Could this be because married people are less sure now of who they are, of what is expected of them in their marriages, and of how to assess their priorities?

In the earlier years of this century people had only one role to fill. A servant in a big house would have done either the cooking or the housework, not both, and the butler certainly wouldn't have been asked to bath the baby! The lady of the house would be expected to look decorative and entertain but not to serve the meal as well, while a poorer married woman, though she had many jobs to do, would not have been expected to go to work and also be a social hostess. The modern woman not only feels pressure to be a perfect mother, housekeeper, cook, lover and hostess, and hold down a job outside the home, but she may also feel that society expects her to fight against the biblical guidelines for husbands and wives.

Sauce for the goose, sauce for the gander

I do not believe that, when the Bible exhorts wives to respect their husbands and husbands to love their wives, the reverse is not also required. Of course wives need to love husbands and husbands to respect wives; but I think that the Bible puts the emphasis in this way so that a husband will not try to subject his wife without being ruled by love for her, and so that a wife will look for aspects of her husband to respect in order to make it easier to acknowledge his leadership. It is very hurtful for either sex to know that their partner does not love or does not respect them. We may feel that the words, 'Oh darling, I do respect you!' sound rather odd compared with a declaration of love, but if we can't bring ourselves to put our feeling of respect into words, at least we can try to show that it is there.

If you are truly concerned for your partner, you should have no trouble in taking a 'do as you would be done by' attitude to your life together. You know that you would worry if your husband stayed out two hours longer than expected without phoning, so you don't do it yourself. You wouldn't want him (or he, you) to spend £50 on a new coat while you're both saving up for a carpet so you don't buy one in those circumstances either. I recently heard a discussion about an all-female Christmas outing to a restaurant which also had a disco; apparently a couple of women had backed out because their husbands didn't want them to go to a disco alone. 'I can't understand that,' said one of the group, 'because I go where I like.' I, on the other hand, could understand and sympathise, because I wouldn't want my husband to go to a disco without me, nor would I expect him to want me to go alone. Certainly a couple may agree to go their separate ways and do as they like with no recriminations, but is that truly a marriage?

Some people don't like the idea of even considering a man's or woman's place within the marriage or the home. They say, 'A woman's place is where she wants it to be, and a man's is where he wants.' This may well be true while we are single (although a Christian single man or woman should also consider where God wants them to be): we can choose to come and go as we please, to live where we choose, to get a job that is secure, dangerous, well-paid or demanding, to come home in the evening or eat out, to have the television on all day or not even to have one. However, people who wish to retain that freedom should remain single, for a man and woman cannot become one flesh and cleave to each other without facing their responsibilities to their partner and the implications of sharing every aspect of their lives.

One of these responsibilities is recognising your partner's needs, and trying to allow him or her to be the person God intends, and also modifying your own involvement in outside activities so that this doesn't adversely affect your marriage. Obviously you should consult your husband if you are thinking of taking on some new commitment and should be open to his guidance if he puts forward sensible and reasonable objections, but if he is truly cherishing you, he will also refrain from becoming involved in extra activities without talking it over first. It is very difficult to strike a balance between 'doing our own thing' and devoting enough time to our marriage, and this problem will be discussed later in the book; at this stage we are considering it from the point of view of a husband and wife being equally aware of each other's needs and fitting these into the biblical order for marriage.

Clare is a young woman who tends to get depressed if she feels she is not busy enough, but her husband Geoff usually objects to her taking on more responsibilities, protesting that she will get too tired. In spite of Geoff's genuine concern for his wife's health he is failing to understand her basic needs, and since he is also unwilling to give up any of his many interests and activities in order to spend more time with her, his constant busy-ness only gives her an increasing desire to be more occupied herself. God has placed the husband at the head of the family (Ephesians 5.23), but you are likely to give only grudging headship to your husband if his attitude is selfish and inconsistent. On the other hand, you should try not to say, 'Because my husband doesn't love and cherish me in a Christ-like way, I am not going to submit to his leadership'. Selwyn Hughes, in *Marriage as God Intended*, claims that a Christian man acquires more of these characteristics as he sees that his wife wants to be submissive.

God's order

At this point I can imagine that you will be protesting, 'Is this going to be another book about the submissive role of the wife? Isn't there more to marriage than that?' The answer is that there is a lot more to marriage, and a lot of problems are caused by quite different aspects of it, but the biblical requirements for husbands and wives are pretty basic and it is therefore appropriate to discuss them in the first chapter. As for the word 'submission', I had hoped to discover that this would only be found in the Authorised Version, and that the newer translations would have something more acceptable. However, most of the new translations continue to use it. The expression 'be subject to' is used in both RSV and NEB. Unfortunately submission and subjection have very distasteful connotations – one thinks of wrestlers using pain to force their opponents into submission, or of a country's citizens being in subjection to a despotic ruler. J. B. Phillip's 'adapt yourself to' is perhaps a happier translation, though not very specific.

Of course, God doesn't want a wife to be subject to a cruel and insensitive husband who rules his family with a rod of iron, or one who will lead her away from the Lord and make her go against her conscience in order to obey him. In Ephesians 5.22–25 we read,

> Wives, submit to your husbands *as to the Lord*. For the husband is the head of the wife as Christ is the head of the church, his body, of which he is the Saviour. Now as the church submits to Christ, so also wives should submit to their husbands in everything. Husbands, love your

4

wives, just as Christ loved the church and gave himself up for her . . .

The command for the husband is the harder one; he has to show both sacrificial love and spirit-controlled leadership in order to love his wife as Christ loved the Church.

The wife should have the relationship to her husband that the Church has to Christ and believe that his leadership is in her best interests because she knows that he loves her: submission which is not prompted by love will lead only to resentment. Christine married young and was very submissive to her husband Tim, not because of the biblical commandment (for they weren't Christians) but because he expected it and she was afraid of him. After a while, however, she began to realise that he was getting everything his own way, so resentment grew and festered and the marriage ended in divorce. Married for the second time, both partners now being Christians, Christine says she is no longer a doormat, though she still regards her husband as the head of the household.

The problem, of course, with applying the biblical guideline, is that the husband is *not* Christ and he cannot have perfect love; the wife knows this and may have reservations about always respecting his decisions. When John and I got married, I have to admit that we left the word 'obey' out of the wedding service; I didn't want to make the promise because I felt I wouldn't keep it, and John was happy about this because he didn't want to carry the responsibility for my actions as well as his own. In the early years he found it very difficult to assume any leadership, and I became increasingly domineering, often making big decisions which should have been his. Fortunately I learned to understand the passage on submission in its true sense, and we were able to discuss it together. John realised that there were some things for which he must take the ultimate responsibility, and as he began to do so I was able to make an effort to leave matters in his hands; when I got used to this I had to admit that it was actually a relief and I did not feel that my intellectual standing was at all diminished.

Making decisions is a terribly difficult area of marriage because it is human nature to say, 'I told you so' if your partner appears to have made a wrong choice. You may feel that your husband's headship of the home is a great privilege and you are entitled to complain if he doesn't exercise it wisely; however, remember that carrying responsibility for a family is not always an enviable task. Part of the responsibility of a caring husband is to weigh his wife's views and perhaps decide to implement them instead of his own; but if he does, he must make the decision his, and not blame her if things go wrong. Jill and Keith found it difficult to decide whether to have their child vaccinated against whooping-cough when there was a dispute about it in medical circles; she acknowledged that he should take the ultimate decision, but knew that she must not throw it back at him if it proved to be the wrong one.

Of course, some decisions are so small that there will be a tacit agreement that the husband can make them without consulting his wife, or in some areas he will delegate the decision-making to her; possibly some would have done so in the example above. There is nothing unscriptural about this, nor about the attitude taken by many couples that they are a partnership and make all decisions jointly. But the happy couple who can do this without dispute and without recriminations is rare, and it is when a conflict occurs that they need to remember that it is the husband who holds ultimate authority before God for his family. The Christian couple, of course, has God to guide every aspect of their lives, and they may find that he has different plans for them than either had thought of. This is an easy answer to the decision-making dilemma, provided that you both accept the guidance. We shall look at this again in chapter 7.

Equality or uniformity?
It's interesting to ask ourselves how different God really intended the roles of men and women to be. We can gain

some insight into this by considering how he made us. We know from Galatians 3.26–29 that God regards men and women as having equal status (as indeed they should also have in the eyes of the law) but this does not mean that they are the same. If God had wanted a world full of identical sexless creatures, he would surely not have made us male and female. There are physiological variations, due to hormones, which tend to make men more aggressive and women more protective. This is something which cannot be disguised however we try to play down the differences by adopting unisex clothing and attitudes. An American researcher noticed that although his students all looked alike from the back view, he could tell their sex by the fact that the women held their books in protective fashion to their breasts, while the men carried theirs more aggressively by their sides!

God wants us to accept and rejoice in the sexuality he has given us, but the great variety in his creation is an indication that we should not let ourselves be stereotyped. We must each find our own level of masculinity or femininity. A husband need not feel inferior because he is not strong and hairy with an aggressively macho image; God's main requirement of a married man is simply that he should submit to the responsibility of providing for his family and of loving and protecting his wife and children (if any). Nor need a wife feel less of a woman because she is physically stronger than average, is not desperately attracted to babies, or is happier in jeans than a frilly skirt; her main requirement is to submit to her husband's leadership and allow him to provide her with spiritual and emotional security. If you have difficulty coming to terms with your masculinity or femininity and the role of your sex, you will find a wide range of help on the bookshelves, for instance, in Elisabeth Elliot's books, *Let me be a Woman* and *The Mark of a Man*.

The obvious biological differences between men and women have no doubt been responsible for the different roles they have assumed in society. In days when families were large, and keeping house was a full-time job, it was natural that the man would be the permanent provider because the woman was the one who produced and breastfed the children. This still applies to the extent that if a woman has a baby she needs time off work, and if she wants to breastfeed she must keep the baby with her. It seems therefore more logical that if a couple is in this situation it is normally the woman who should remain at home as long as the child or children need someone to care for them full-time.

This does not mean, however, that a wife has no function outside the home or the husband no place in it. I have suggested that the woman might stay at home for a while if she has a baby, because that is in keeping with the way God has made her body; if, however, she is childless, or her children no longer need constant attention, there is certainly no biblical reason for her to be tied to a life of domesticity. Note the 'good wife' in Proverbs 31, whose diverse activities were by no means all concerned with homemaking but whose husband and children did not suffer as a result.

It is also important to note that although God made us with different bodies, he gave men and women equal intelligence, creativity and appreciation of the arts; so it is quite wrong to suggest that a woman should not feel the need of a career or other fulfilling pastime, just as her husband does. If you are a woman who is successful in your career, you may find it difficult to submit (I wish we could use another word!) to your husband if his job is less exalted than yours, and you will both need to remember that God's order for the family applies regardless of the intelligence or achievements of either partner. The husband is the spiritual head, not necessarily the family Mastermind; and if you have a superior brain to his you should both be able to benefit from the contributions you will make to family discussions before he takes the ultimate decisions. A husband whose wife gives up a job she enjoys in order to look after small children or perhaps an invalid, should realise that she may be feeling just as frustrated as he would in a similar situation. He can show that he still respects her as a person by trying to make it possible for her to carry on any work or hobby that she finds fulfilling.

Who does what?

Some people believe that if one partner has to remain at home, there is no more reason for it to be the wife than the husband. They advocate the freedom to reverse roles completely, so that the wife is the sole provider and the husband's function is to keep house and look after the children. I have tried to make it clear that I do not agree with this because I don't think it is what God intended; moreover it would be much harder for a husband to become involved in the activities which are available for people at home unless there were many other men in the same position. The situation is different if a husband is at home, not as housekeeper or childminder, but because he wants to try an alternative workstyle, such as free-lance writing or painting, or setting up a small business, while his wife brings in a regular income. God created a man with the basic instinct of being provider and with the injunction to be the head of the family, and he should at least feel that he is trying to provide for his family, even if the work he has chosen is not yet bringing in enough money.

Some men, of course, think that it reflects badly on their ability to provide if their wife goes out to work. Such an attitude is unreasonable, since it presupposes that a wife only wants to go out to work to earn money and discounts her God-given intelligence and desire to exercise her gifts and also her need to interact with other people.

It is not uncommon, nowadays, for a husband to become unemployed, and if his wife is already in a well-paid job it would obviously seem ridiculous for her to give up. She will then have to be the one who is sensitive to the frustration her husband is feeling and to the need to show continuing respect for him even though he is temporarily unable to be the main provider. A husband in this position may find it helpful not to slip entirely into the role of 'house-husband' but to fill his time with constructive work at home (for

9

example in decorating or growing vegetables), to try to get involved in voluntary work, or even to explore the possibility of becoming self-employed.

If your husband loses his job at a time when you are at home looking after young children, should you try to get work while he acts as child-minder? Such an arrangement would obviously ease the financial problems, and you might find there was less tension in the home if you were not under each other's feet all day. There could also be positive advantages, in that you would have a welcome break from being tied to the house, while your husband would gain an insight into the pressures of your everyday life. However, unless you feel that God is calling you to permanent role reversal, it is important that you see this as a temporary arrangement. Your husband should retain a positive attitude as he seeks work and not feel demoralised that you have found employment more easily than he has.

In the case of Denise and Alastair, the wife felt it would be wrong to go out to work in these circumstances. She had recently become a Christian, and her husband had left her and then returned, although he had no job. Finances were very difficult and Denise knew it would be quite possible for her to get a job while Alastair was at home with their little boy. However, she was determined to make their marriage work and to let her husband start to be the head of the family; she felt that this would not be possible if she became the breadwinner even for a short time. Happily, things turned out well, and although it was many months before Alastair found a job, their marriage improved. After a while he too became a Christian and they were then able to slip much more easily into God's guidelines for Christian husbands and wives.

Male chauvinism
Possibly one reason why many women today find it hard to accept the 'submissive' role is that the inferior status of women in years gone by has been bound up with a great deal of male chauvinism. This is often typified by the man

who treats his home like a hotel, makes no effort to share in the household tasks, and escapes to the pub at every opportunity. You would not expect a Christian husband to behave like that, but unfortunately there is a Christian version of male chauvinism in which both partners feel that the wife should take full responsibility for all that goes on at home, regardless of the circumstances. Judy was expecting her fifth child and suffering bad health as the pregnancy progressed; this was made worse by constant worry that household chores wouldn't get done and things wouldn't be ready for the baby. She felt so strongly that her place was in the home and her husband's was not, that they didn't feel the freedom for him to share the jobs and reduce some of her burden.

Such an inflexible attitude is obviously not very sensible; and in any case, a husband who feels that he should not be concerned with the running of the home or the care of the children, is making it virtually impossible for his wife to choose to get an outside job. It is a very heavy burden for a woman to go out to work as well as doing the cooking, cleaning, washing, shopping, and so on, single-handed. It is even worse if there are children's needs to be catered for as well.

Many couples have a sort of 'sliding scale' of involvement in household tasks, depending on who is going out to work and what the commitments are at home. For example, they may have shared the household jobs equally when both were in full-time work, and then the wife may take on a greater portion when she stays at home with young children, so that her husband has more time in the evenings to devote to the little ones and to her. Or if she is having a difficult time perhaps with a new baby, or has taken on a part-time job as well, he needs to do as much as possible to lessen her burden in the evenings and at weekends, so that she can have time to herself and to spend with him.

Some couples agree that, if they have children, the wife should stay home for a while and keep house but when the time comes for her to want to return to work, her husband has got out of the habit of being much involved in the daily chores and says she can get a job only if things at home aren't affected. Although this sounds selfish, it may not be an unreasonable attitude if he has a very time-consuming job as well as responsibilities at church; he could feel that if he starts sharing the housework he will have no time to devote to his wife or children, so that family life will suffer. The obvious answer, if you are in this position, is to use part of your increased income employing someone to do some of the housework. In this way, you can both get job satisfaction and can both have time to devote to the family. If you have no children, and both have demanding jobs, you may also find this is the best solution, as it will allow you the time and energy to spend together and with other people.

Wanting your home to run smoothly and your wife to have time to spend with you is not male chauvinism; expecting it to happen without any involvement from you, is. Many men inherit this attitude from their fathers who were never seen to help in the house, either because of the long hours spent at work or because both they and their wives considered it degrading for them to do it. Women can be guilty of adding to the problem by expecting only their daughters to help in the house, while waiting on their sons hand and foot; this obviously makes it difficult for a young man to adapt to marriage if his wife is not willing to continue this treatment! Fortunately, some men (like my husband) have managed to break out of this hereditary mould, and this should augur well for the next generation, who will begin to accept it as the norm for men to get involved in the household tasks. My two elder boys have found it quite acceptable to push their brothers in the pram, and the little ones actually have a toy pushchair; this is because they have always seen their father taking the baby for a walk – if they copied their grandfathers they would not be doing it!

When a husband and father takes on a role of responsible leadership in the home, his sons will expect to do this in their own families and his daughters will look for husbands who can fulfil this role. A Christian mother should make it clear to her children that their father is the head of the family and should encourage them to go to both parents for decisions, even though – if she spends most of her time looking after them – they may be inclined to look upon her as the source of authority. The ultimate authority, of course, is God, and to adhere to his guidelines for the family and for marriage makes as much sense as following the maker's instructions on anything we buy. The ideas put forward in the rest of this book are therefore based unashamedly on God's plan, while acknowledging that, though it is the best way, it is not always the easiest.

Questions to ask

Do the unpleasant connotations of the word 'submit' make it difficult for you to accept the teaching in Ephesians 5?

In what ways do you show your partner that you respect, as well as love, him (or her)?

If you have children, would you be happy for them to copy your own roles when they get married?

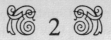

2

What's Yours is Mine . . .

'. . . and what's mine's my own' is a cynical saying about marriage which my grandmother used to enjoy quoting. There may not be many couples who consciously entertain this selfish attitude; but many embark upon marriage without fully realising that they will have to take someone else's wishes into account regarding spending, saving and giving. Tension can arise in a marriage when decisions have to be made about who does the accounts and who allocates the money, and further strain may be added if children are born and the family income seems inadequate. When John and I were engaged I had an unrealistically rosy view of marriage, but I was aware even then that any major arguments we had would probably be about money, and I was right. Like it or not, many aspects of our lives are directly or indirectly affected by the amount of money we have and our attitude to it.

Joint or separate?
Probably one of the first decisions to be made is how many bank accounts to have. Many couples, even though they believe in sharing their money, like to have separate accounts (or separate allocations if it is all done on a cash basis). Some women have their own accounts even when they are not working, for instance, Janet's husband pays a proportion of his salary into her account for housekeeping. She uses this to buy food, clothes, and so on, and does what she likes with any surplus. He pays the bills out of the rest of the money. In this way they know that they are always

14

able to live off one income. When Janet earns any money, it goes into her account and they discuss what to do with it – buy a new carpet, perhaps, or take a holiday.

Other couples I know who are both earning, also have separate accounts but operate a slightly more haphazard system: they simply compare bank statements when the bills come in and decide who pays, trusting that one of them will be able to! Some couples dislike the idea of joint accounts because they feel they have no money of 'their own' with which to buy their partner a present – indeed it may happen that a quite elderly woman will take a part-time job simply in order to feel that she can have money to spend on presents. This may be a shame if she is married to a man who is generous and wants his wife to feel that they have 'everything in common'.

I have always felt that the idea of a joint account is a good one for a marriage; if there is complete sharing it is appropriate for all the income to go into a common fund, and if there is perfect trust, neither should mind the other looking at the cheque stubs! If the wife gives up working, she still has access to the account and is able to see her contribution to the budget as being in kind – performing services that would otherwise have to be paid for. She can draw money out as freely as her husband can, and doesn't have to feel she must ask him whenever she needs more. John and I do not have a set amount for housekeeping but buy what we need as it is necessary, sometimes bulk-buying for the freezer. Consulting the cheque book tells us whether we need to cut down on spending in general, or whether a large purchase should be deferred till the next month.

One hears dreadful stories about one partner being landed with the other's debts when a marriage breaks up, and about terrible squabbles over possessions, so it is not surprising that those who have experienced such traumas should be wary of joint accounts. However, the important thing is not how many bank accounts you choose to have, but your attitude to what goes into them. A husband who takes on the role of main breadwinner should recognise the significance of all the jobs his wife does in the home and therefore feel able to share with her the freedom to spend 'his' money. A wife who returns to work should not expect to keep her new wealth to herself, but should share it, as her husband has shared his with her over the years.

Who holds the purse strings?
If one partner has to give up work and remain at home I have assumed that it will be the wife, while the husband will act as main breadwinner. However, this does not necessarily mean that he will control the money. In some households, a man hands his weekly pay-packet to his wife on returning home and she gives him some back as 'pocket money'. In a family where a monthly salary is paid, it may still be the wife who writes cheques for the bills and tell her husband how much he can spend.

Having assumed the biblical standpoint that the husband is the head of the house, we then have to consider whether he needs to hold the purse strings in order to maintain this status. I would say, for our own marriage, that he does; to me the responsibility of paying bills and keeping accounts would be one of the biggest problems of single life, and I am only too pleased to hand over the task to my husband and accept his leadership in organising the finances. This is because I have a somewhat neurotic attitude towards money; I hate to talk about it and I never open bills. So, although the image of a feeble protected wife is not very appealing, I have to admit that I enjoy being protected from financial worries.

This system works well for us, because John is well suited to managing the money, having the mind of an accountant, and he wouldn't want me to do it, even if I were willing. Other couples, however, operate the other way round; the husband has no idea about organising the finances, while the wife is a skilled bookkeeper. Colin and Philippa are such a couple; she pays all the bills and keeps household accounts, and presumably if Colin were paid weekly in cash he would hand over his pay-packet so that she could do this.

16

When challenged with the suggestion that their system is perhaps not scriptural, Philippa defends it by saying that the managing director of a company never does the accounts himself, but employs someone else to do it. When Colin wants to consider spending money, he asks his 'accountant' how much is available, and then makes his decision. In this way they feel that he remains head of the house and she is performing a task for him – like ironing his shirts.

Certainly it would seem stupid, if God has given the ability to a woman and withheld it from a man, for the husband to keep muddling through against his will. What really matters is the attitude to money management; if a couple are allowing the woman's control of the money to turn into control of the home and of their relationship, then something is wrong. Each of us has to find the system that suits us best, and then try to apply it with generosity and understanding. If you let your husband take the full burden of managing the finances, you shouldn't adopt an irresponsible attitude and spend money like water – and then expect him to sort things out! A husband who doles out a housekeeping allowance should make himself aware of the ever rising prices and try to allow enough. You should both think twice before asking the other to write down everything they spend; this could be a tremendous burden to some people.

Materialism

But why does money have to be such a big issue in many marriages? I think it is because society in general is so money-orientated: I don't just mean the pressure to buy the expensive luxuries which are so persuasively advertised, but also the fact that money plays a dominant role everywhere. Jobs are advertised for the salary they command rather than the satisfaction they offer; political parties ask for your money more frequently than for your vote; charities generally appeal for money rather than practical help. Many churches, too, will appeal for money to repair the spire, build a new hall, or support the current mission, and new

Christians receive teaching on the importance of 'good stewardship', which is evangelical jargon for allocating your money sensibly.

It is therefore not surprising that the question of how to spend our money (or how to make more if we can't manage on what we have) can appear to be a very important one. Even if we are determined not to be selfishly materialistic, there is still the feeling that we could do so much more good if we had more money. And this is true, because there are so many things we cannot do without money. Travelling by car or bus is expensive, so that will curtail visiting sick or lonely people unless it is possible to walk or cycle. Postage, and the cost of cards and using the telephone, can mount up, and this can be a problem to people who like to cheer their friends up with a letter or phone call or send 'get well' cards. Some may feel they have the gift of hospitality and though they may acknowledge that an expensive meal is not necessary, if money is tight even coffee and biscuits all round can make a different to the budget. Those who want to offer longer-term hospitality will be better able to do so if they can afford a house with a spare room.

Standard of living
The question of how much a couple – or an individual – actually needs to live on is really not possible to answer, because when we look at the standard of living in developing countries we realise that perhaps many things we class as necessities in Western Europe are really luxuries. Although we should not ignore the fact that a certain amount of spending on ourselves and our families, for presents, outings, celebration meals and so on, is important to increase the quality our our lives together, we need to be careful to bring up our children to be aware of those so much worse off.

The amount of spending that goes on at Christmas is particularly inappropriate, and this is a good time for Christian couples to show that giving in the wider sense can be as important as giving expensive presents to each other and the children. Even so, there can be tension in a marriage if, for instance, one partner feels that they ought to buy their child a new bike like all his friends have, while the other feels it would be quite wrong to spend so much in this way.

Everyone needs holidays, but some holidays are extravagant by any standards. A few years ago, the opportunity arose for John and me to go with a group of Christians to Israel. We were concerned about whether it was right to spend so much (even if we did regard it as a pilgrimage rather than a holiday), until suddenly I received several hundred pounds as an unexpected legacy. We then felt it was right to go and have never regretted it, especially as it was the last time we were able to go away as a couple before having our third and fourth children.

It is very easy to confuse something we want to do with what we think God wants for us. Malcolm and Hazel believed that God was leading them to a larger house, and they took on a mortgage which was really bigger then they could cope with. Soon Malcolm was suggesting that Hazel should go out to work, even though they had two very young children, and this placed a strain on their marriage, particularly as they had also moved a few miles away from their church and their Christian friends, which meant that when they started to have problems they lacked the support of Christian fellowship. Of course, it is right for some people to have big houses and use them for the Lord, but it is important to be very sure of God's guidance if it seems that the move will leave insufficient money for normal family life.

Standard of giving
Many Christians who are short of money still feel able to give generously to the Lord's work and to charity, and for this reason they may not be any better off than their neighbours who spend a lot of money at the pub or the betting shop. What is strange, however, is that Christian families who give money away and live reasonably simply

all seem to survive on different levels of income. It is probable that Parkinson's Law applies and that one's 'needs' expand to fit one's income. It can cause problems in a marriage, though, when one partner points to another couple living on far less, and criticises the other for needing more. Trouble can also arise if a large sum of money is inherited and you disagree about whether to give it away, go on a world cruise, or pay off the mortgage.

Even when we try to be much less materialistic, and to be generous in giving, there may be conflict in marriage because there are several different ways of giving money away, and one person's character may be more suited to one kind of giving than other. In *We Believe in Marriage*, Elizabeth Goldsmith points out that she often feels the need to give spontaeously to an urgent need, while her husband prefers to give strategically, if possible by convenant, so that the recipient can claim the income tax back. Recognising that these feelings stemmed from their different personalities, they agreed to covenant the bulk of their money but reserve some for her to dip into when she felt it right.

Where one of you is a Christian and the other is not, great sensitivity is needed. Those who provide training for new Christians are often quick to teach the importance of tithing and other forms of giving, but slow to recognise the problems this can cause with a non-Christian partner. Most often it is the wife who is converted first; if she is to let her husband retain (or take on) his role of leadership, it is not really appropriate for her to start giving away large chunks of their money to her church or her favourite missionary society. When Pauline became a Christian she really latched on to the teaching about giving. As they had two little boys, her husband Mark's wages had been supporting the family. Pauline then managed to get a part-time job at some inconvenience to the family, and she regarded all her earnings as 'her' money to give away. Although it was very laudable for Pauline to be willing to give away everything she earned, Mark might have been excused for thinking that she should have shared her earnings as he had been sharing his with her – (particularly as they had always been short of money).

There are, of course, other decisions to be made regarding giving money away: if you can agree how, and how much, you must also decide what to give to. Brian felt it was his duty to support their church, but his wife Lynne was unhappy about giving large amounts to the church because she felt the money was often wasted on substantial and unnecessary items. She would have preferred all that money to go to relief agencies. Lynne also sometimes liked to donate to secular charities, while Brian said they should leave the non-Christians to do that. Very often Lynne would withdraw from discussions on giving and allow Brian to exercise his leadership and make all the decisions. This avoided overt conflict, but it would have been better if Brian and Lynne could have prayed together about their giving and come to some agreement, so that Lynne could have felt as much a part of it as he was.

Just for a rainy day
Another aspect of money, which can vie with both giving and spending, is saving. Elizabeth Goldsmith writes of being confronted with the decision whether to put aside some money to help the children set up a home in the future, or to give it away to famine relief work in India. She felt that this tension from time to time was a good thing, because it forced them to remember that their money belonged to God and turn to him for guidance. In some marriages, however, tension of this kind leads only to a strained relationship, and it is difficult for one partner to accept guidance if it is in conflict with what he or she was taught as a child.

Some Christians believe fervently that the requirement to 'take no thought for the morrow' means that it is wrong to have savings of any kind, and therefore that any surplus money should be spent or given away. It is very difficult to live with someone like that when you know that a large

21

amount of money could suddenly be needed for a repair bill, or a new car, or to cope with some unexpected disaster! On the other hand, some Christians feel it right to save money for their children, if not for themselves. Others believe that good stewardship means putting aside enough to cover all reasonable eventualities in order to avoid ever getting into debt. Some feel it is right to get the maximum tax relief, and do this by keeping the largest mortgage they can afford, but one Christian man I knew, who was certainly not poor, refused to go to the expense of having a telephone in the house until the whole mortgage had been paid off.

Insurance is another difficult question. Of course, some kinds, like car insurance, are compulsory; but others may seem like gambling. In two of my pregnancies we insured against twins, not because we didn't want them, but because it would have cost us a lot more money if we had had them. A Christian doctor friend criticised this attitude, but I have since met other Christians who have done the same thing. Pension schemes and life assurance can be a great comfort to those who like to have security for the future. Some Christians, on the other hand, feel it is wrong to store up large amounts of 'treasure on earth' in this way. There is no one right or wrong answer; we must each agree on what is right for us.

On the receiving end
Many people, including Christians, spend so much time working to make more money that they have no time to benefit from it; it is easy for them to say they would be happier without the money, but no one should make such a claim unless they have actually experienced the hardships of poverty. Those who have had to cope with lack of money may have little sympathy with the 'problems' of people who cannot agree on how to dispose of their wealth. Some couples, like Martin and Elizabeth Goldsmith, find that the struggle and the need to rely on the Lord have brought them closer together, but for others a heavy strain is put on the marriage in times of financial crisis.

The position is different, of course, when your lack of money arises not from unemployment or the low income 'poverty trap' but because you are doing Christian work which involves 'living by faith' – in other words receiving no payment, only gifts from those who support your work. To be able to trust the Lord for every penny requires a greater than average faith (possibly the special gift mentioned in 1 Corinthians 12.9), and it would be disastrous to attempt it unless you were both united in exercising trust. The decision to enter this type of Christian service can also be difficult because it involves swallowing your pride and being willing to receive money as a gift – you are given money by God's people because you are doing his work.

If, however, your shortage of money arises from redundancy, from the need to change to a less lucrative job, from illness, or is the result of a decision to re-train for a new career, it is even harder to accept that other people should contribute to your support. It is quite common practice to hand on children's clothes, prams, bicycles, etc., even when no financial hardship is involved, or to share garden produce with friends or bake a cake for a sick person. These forms of sharing are more acceptable because they can usually be reciprocated at some other time. Somehow a gift of money is a greater blow to the pride than a gift in kind. A verse which is often used to encourage reluctant givers to part with their money is, 'It is more blessed to give than to receive' (Acts 20.35), and this sometimes makes people feel uncomfortable about receiving. Of course, no one can obtain the blessing of giving unless someone is willing to receive, but since the recipient can so easily be a worthy charity, many people think that there is no need for an individual to become willing to accept money.

So how does this affect marriage? As with everything else, it will only be a problem if you and your partner disagree on what you should receive, and since it is such a touchy subject it is very likely that you will. I am not referring to situations in which you pray together for the £50 you desperately need and then a mysterious cheque arrives in the post, but to times when you might have gifts of money or other things handed to you out of the blue.

The Christian man who believes that it is his responsibility to try to support his family, will often be the one who feels insulted if money – or even second-hand clothes – are offered, and his wife will need to understand that this can be a blow to his pride and his ego. If this is true of your husband, you may have to be willing to resist the gift however much you feel your family needs what has been offered. You will be able to do this without offence, as the giver will know that you are only refusing because of your husband. If you feel strongly about it, you can pray that he will reach the point of being able to accept charity.

It can happen the other way round, however, particularly if you have been brought up to believe that offering money is a terrible insult, or if you feel that your husband is accepting charity rather than making an effort to work. Jonathan had chosen to change his employment, with a subsequent drop in salary, which required financial adjustment, though no actual hardship. One day at a prayer meeting he accepted a small gift of money from a friend and went home rejoicing because – as he saw it – the Lord was looking after their needs. His wife Heather was horrified that he had accepted it, not just because her pride was hurt, but also because it seemed totally wrong to take a sum of money that they didn't specifically need at that moment (since it wouldn't have paid any of the bills) from people who were living on less than they were. Jonathan still wanted his family to have occasional outings and some luxuries, but Heather felt that they could only justify receiving hand-outs from people who lived very simply if they themselves lived on the bare essentials. Perhaps she should have been more willing to accept Jonathan's leadership and not criticise the way he brought money into the home, but as he knew it would be a problem to her it might have been better if he had accepted the gift without telling her.

Heather had been brought up to believe that, except

within the family, giving and receiving money and expensive gifts was totally unacceptable, and she had not been able to outgrow this idea. If she wanted to give money to a friend in need she would do so anonymously to avoid embarrassment. Jonathan's parents were also very proud of their financial independence, but his journey in the Christian faith had enabled him to move on from that standpoint and be willing to sink his pride if he felt it necessary: he even felt it right to receive simply to give others the joy of giving.

Many of the financial problems and tensions discussed in this chapter stem from upbringing. John and I have had difficulties in our own marriage because we come from families with very different views on money. A person whose childhood was one of 'make do and mend' will be bound to be affected by this attitude, either to copy it or to go to the other extreme. Anyone lucky enough to have been brought up in an affluent home will have difficulty adjusting to a tight budget, and a child who has seen his parents financially ruined by ill-health or unscrupulous contacts will be unlikely to want to take risks himself. In all aspects of marriage we carry with us the memories of childhood and the values and characteristics of the people who bore us – so for that reason we must move in and tackle the thorny question of the in-laws!

Questions to ask

In what ways are the arrangements you have made for managing your money consistent – or inconsistent – with the husband being the head of the house?

Are you giving away as much as your conscience tells you that you should?

If God has blessed you with money and material possessions, how can you use them to serve him better?

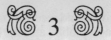

3

In-laws or Out-laws

On many occasions I have talked to people, either singly or in groups, about the subject matter of this book, and whenever I mention the word 'in-laws' there is nearly always an audible groan. It seems that the antipathy towards mothers-in-law did not die with the music hall jokes which caricatured them, and in some families they are very much the 'out-laws'.

It is not surprising that so many problems arise, because the in-law relationship is such an artificial one. Our natural family can often be difficult to live with, too, what with sibling rivalry, the generation gap, teenage rebellion and so on, but over the years we have grown used to our own family and they have accepted us with all our faults; we choose our friends, and our marriage partner, because we are attracted to them, and share common interests. There is no family or friendship bond between us and our in-laws, yet we are expected to be just as close to them emotionally. In some families the tension and outright hostility may mean that there is no answer except to keep your distance and pray for what would virtually be a miracle (and such miracles do happen!) of repaired relationships. However, it may be useful to look at some of the things that can be gained from in-laws, and the causes of some of the problems.

Not good enough?
The first hurdle to be overcome is the reaction of our beloved's parents when marriage is first mentioned. Young people, who have no responsibilities, and who have spent

twenty or so years thinking about themselves, tend to be basically selfish (yes, even Christians!) and if they are seriously in love all their thoughts and emotions will be centred on the relationship. It is likely, therefore, that they will be particularly sensitive to any adverse reaction they may pick up from their potential in-laws, and will find it difficult to look at things from their point of view.

If the young couple are Christians and have prayed about their future and believe that God wants them to marry, they may feel that all questions of, 'Are you really suited?', 'Do you know him/her well enough?' or 'How will you live?' are quite irrelevant. It may be that they are right to go ahead and follow God's leading, but that is no reason for brushing aside the parents' natural concern about practical matters. It would be a better witness, if they were to show themselves to be caring and responsible and were ready to discuss their future plans, than if they disregarded their parents' concern with a sort of spiritual snobbery.

Some parents genuinely do feel that the fiancé(e) is not good enough for their child, whether socially, intellectually, morally or spiritually, and this is obviously very hurtful to the young person concerned. It is also very sad, because it may for ever poison the relationship. A married person in later life might say resignedly, 'Of course, I never really got on with Jane's parents, she was an only child, and they didn't think I was good enough for her.' Until recently I had little sympathy with this parental attitude, but now that I can envisage assessing my own sons' girlfriends in a few years time, I can begin to understand how it can arise.

A greater problem still is faced by parents who had set their hearts on their child marrying a family friend or former boy– or girlfriend. We know that we cannot arrange marriages in our culture, but that doesn't stop us having daydreams! The most helpful thing you can do if you are newly-engaged is to make every effort to get close to your fiancé's parents and get to know them well before they become in-laws.

Once the engagement has been announced, the next

hurdle to be overcome is the wedding plans, and it is at this fence that many relationships with potential in-laws (and indeed with one's own parents) can stumble and take a long time to recover. Everyone feels nervy and sensitive just before a wedding, and little disagreements and difficulties that would be shrugged off in normal circumstances, assume an unwarranted importance. At this stage a young couple can feel that they are being 'piggy-in-the-middle' between two sets of warring parents, and it is no wonder that some have wished they could just elope. Perhaps this is a problem that will decrease now that many couples are getting married later, with the parents assuming less financial responsibility for the wedding.

A surprisingly large number of people seem to have trouble deciding what to call their in-laws, and I think that the form of address you choose may be indicative of the relationship between you. If you are fortunate enough to feel nearly as close to your partner's parents as you do to your own, you will have no difficulty calling them 'Mum and Dad', whereas if you see them more as friends than parents you will probably use Christian names. In the less happy families, where relations are distant, the older couple may even continue to be addressed as 'Mr and Mrs . . . '. The arrival of children often makes the situation easier, because then everyone can say 'Grandpa and Grandma'.

Loyalties

A major problem occurs when you feel you are in the centre of a stuggle between your partner and your parents or your parents-in-law. The fortunate ones are people like Veronica, whose in-laws (even though they weren't Christians) disapproved of her because her previous husband had left her and she was divorced. Veronica's second husband defended her from the start, and although he kept in close touch with his family and was supportive to them, he never took their side against hers.

It is not surprising that the question of loyalty can be very difficult for we have spent so many years honouring, obeying

28

and being loyal to our parents. However, the Bible does say quite clearly that 'a man will leave his father and mother and be united to his wife, and they will become one flesh' (Genesis 2.24), which is not inconsistent with continuing to honour his parents (Exodus 20.2). It is therefore necessary to give total support to the partner you have chosen, not only in the face of society, but in the face of your parents. It is, in fact, good if this situation arises before marriage, because if you then find it impossible to transfer loyalty from your parents to your fiancé, you should break off the engagement. In this respect, I always think it is sad when married people talk about their parents' house or the area in which they were brought up as 'home'. It would be good to try to restrict the word 'home' to the place where husband and wife live together.

Loyalty also means not complaining to your parents about your partner – be it over work in the house, use of money, attitude to the church or anything else – and trying not to compare your husband to your father (or your wife to your mother). It means, too, not being ready to run home to Mum as soon as things start to go wrong, because this will cause a breach between her and your husband. If you have a close relationship with your mother or father, it may be a temptation to share the frustrations of early married life and to gossip about your partner's faults, but this is certainly not consistent with loyalty, nor is it likely to foster a good relationship between your partner and your parents. (On the other hand, if things have gone so wrong that they are seemingly irreparable, good parents can be a great support and help.)

When Jenny married Julian, she found that her mother-in-law was very domineering, and that Julian was still willing to let her rule his life. Jenny, whose marriage eventually broke up, thinks that this was unscriptural and that a man should put his wife first, and when she remarried she felt that they should start as they meant to go on in their relationship with their parents. She now has an excellent relationship with her new in-laws and is a great help to them in their old age. Putting your partner first doesn't mean prohibiting contact with parents, as in the case of Charles and Marian, whose marriage also broke up. Charles was much older than his wife and quite unreasonable in the restrictions he placed upon her, so that Marian found that if she ever wanted to visit her mother she had to deceive him in order to do so. In her second marriage she was determined to rectify this and to be honest in everything.

Criticism or advice?

If only a young married couple could project themselves forward some thirty years and know how they would react as parents and grandparents, and if only middle-aged parents could remember what it was like to be young and newlywed, there would probably be far fewer problems. Margaret was a woman who suffered greatly from a mother-in-law who interfered and tried to run her life. Fortunately she used this to remind her not to interfere with her own daughters-in-law, even though she was very unhappy about the way one of them was caring for her children. The trouble with learning from your own experiences at the hands of others is that it doesn't seem to benefit you, only the next generation! However, people like Margaret do have the advantage of enjoying a happier relationship with their own sons– and daughters-in-law. This is not to say that the young couple should automatically feel aggrieved every time their parents say something they dislike. While the older couple might have benefited if they had remembered how they felt when they were young, and kept quiet, it is still not sensible to say 'they should know better' and to allow yourself to be deeply offended.

In *Marriage as God Intended*, Selwyn Hughes recognises the problem of trying to be loyal to your partner in the face of criticism from your parents. His helpful advice includes the suggestion that a married man, for example, should refuse to listen or take part when his parents criticise his wife behind her back: he should always politely ask them to wait until she is there so that they can talk it over together.

Parents who have been very protective – this is most likely to happen if they have an only child – are quite likely to be tempted to criticise the young marriage partner and to assume that their child is not being as well looked after as he or she was at home. A young wife is frequently accused of not feeding her husband properly (even though, in fact, he may do much of the cooking!) or not cleaning the house properly, and a husband may be considered to be a bad provider if he is not ambitious in his job. If children are born, a whole new area of conflict can open up. It is not surprising that the older couple will be keenly interested in the upbringing of their grandchildren, as they are their own flesh and blood, and since the grandparents have – by definition – already had children, they may be forgiven for feeling that they have had more experience.

The main thing about advice is that it is much more likely to be taken if it is asked for and not thrust down the throat. It is all too easy for a young mother to react against uninvited advice and automatically reject it as being outdated. Moreover, where young babies are concerned there is so much conflicting advice (even from health visitors) on how often to feed, whether to pick up a crying baby, when to start potty training etc., that it is essential for the new parents to choose their own plan to work by.

Of course, a mother-in-law may be able to put her finger on just what is troubling the fractious baby, and in the most fortunate families she will have such a relationship with her daughter-in-law that the younger woman feels able to ask for advice without risking criticism, and the older woman knows to withhold it until asked. The same principles will also apply to advice from your own parents, although you will usually be more likely to turn to your own mother for help, so there won't be such difficulty with advice being given before it is requested. The problem here could be if you rely too much on your mother's support instead of your partner's.

Relationships with children

Some young couples find that if they have children family relations become easier, because at last they have something in common with their in-laws, and they may have more need to turn to them for help and support. The older couple, perhaps fearing that the marriage wouldn't last, or unable to get over their initial misgivings about their child's partner, may have kept themselves aloof. However, when the first grandchild comes along they think that perhaps some good will come out of the union, and also realise that if they don't get on better terms with the baby's parents they will see very little of the child.

On the other hand, relations between grandparents and children can cause a great deal of tension in a family, not least between the children's parents themselves. As well as the problem of unwanted advice, there are two basic reasons for tension over children. First, the grandparents may try telling the children what to do, disciplining them in a way that is unacceptable to one or both parents. Phil had grown up in a home where his mother worked part-time, and his grandmother, who lived with them, helped to bring him up. When Phil and his wife Tracy had children, Phil's mother naturally assumed that grandmothers should have some say in the upbringing; to Phil this was not unnatural, but to Tracy, whose grandparents had not had that role, it was all wrong.

The second common problem is that of indulging the children. Most people seem to accept that this is part of the role of the grandparent, but it is very difficult for young parents to understand why the people who brought them up with strictly rationed sweets and limited pocket money should suddenly acquire a different attitude when giving to their grandchildren! The worst thing about it, especially when you are trying to bring children up not to be materialistic, is when the gifts become so regular that the children say, 'We're going to see Grandad today. I wonder what we'll get!'

Some of you who are parents may have genuine objections to the sweets or toys or books the grandparents are giving to your children, and if you feel strongly enough, then it may be possible for you to sit down with the older couple and explain your reasons. Again, however, it is useful to try to put yourself in the other person's position: if any of my children grew up to be or to marry atheists, I should not want to be denied the freedom to give their children Christian books. Should I then be less ready to criticise things that are given to my children?

This problem with grandparents can become an area of conflict between a couple if they are not united in their approach to it. Vic's parents were very generous and kept buying sweets, ice creams, etc. for his children, and also encouraged them to eat sugary foods which they weren't given at home. His wife Rachel was annoyed about this, because she felt it undermined the concern she had for the children's teeth and general health. Vic felt that she was making too much of it and therefore wouldn't take her objections seriously. This made Rachel feel that everyone was against her, and she became increasingly worked up about it. All the unpleasantness might have been avoided if they had had a more united front in the first place and if Vic, instead of opting out, had shown that he was on his wife's 'side' while trying to reconcile her to his parents. He could have explained to them that the children were already overweight – which they would have accepted better from him – and that their sugar intake was being controlled, and he could have gently encouraged Rachel to accept more from them – which she might have done if she could have seen that he was supporting her.

This principle applies to larger issues as well. If you feel that your partner is siding with his parents (or anyone else) against you, you will automatically react against him and the others, and thus make the situation worse.

I had some problems with my in-laws, but when they died, there was one thing I learned: you don't always appreciate people until they have gone. I wished then that I had not spent so much time complaining about their views on various things and had been more ready to appreciate the very fact that they were there.

Background
It is sometimes said, when people complain about their loved one's parents, 'Well, it doesn't matter. You're marrying him, not his family.' This is only partly true, because although you shouldn't be put off marrying someone because of the family they come from, it is very stupid to go into marriage with blinkers on, pretending that the in-laws don't exist. Families inevitably come 'as a package'; even though they may not see the younger couple very often and may live hundreds of miles away, parents will always have left something of themselves in their children's emotional make-up. Whether a young person has felt close to his parents and has retained most of their values, or whether he has rebelled and gone the other way, a lot can be learned about the way he reacts by studying the influences on his childhood.

Some couples have such differing backgrounds that their own union could be a disaster if they failed to view each other's behaviour in the light of this. Bob and Penny are a prime example, because their parents exhibited the extremes of over-protectiveness and neglect. Bob, though not an only child, had parents who wanted to organise every aspect of his life. Their genuine love and concern for his wellbeing unfortunately resulted in their forcing him into a career in business when he had the chance to be a professional tennis player. As Bob was an easy-going person, he had allowed them to do this and did not even object when they wanted to know every detail of his financial affairs after he had left home and married.

Bob's childhood problems, however, might seem as nothing compared to Penny's. She was very much the 'mistake', born to ageing parents who had no love left either for each other or their children. During all her years at home she suffered neglect and ill-treatment; she was constantly told that she wasn't wanted, her achievements were belittled, and no interest was taken in anything she did. Before she married, Penny suffered a breakdown, but the fact that she had become a Christian helped her through it, and – amazingly – enabled her to begin to forgive her parents.

Not surprisingly, relations with the in-laws were strained. The couple would never be close to Penny's parents (and she had almost lost touch with her brothers), while Bob's continued to try to dominate him. Although Penny had not enjoyed having neglectful parents, she found it difficult to accept the other extreme and couldn't understand why Bob still let his parents run his life. Although he had known love and stability as a child, he had had no chance to develop qualities of decision-making and responsibility, and he therefore found it difficult to take on a role of leadership in his marriage, much as Penny wanted him to. She had to learn to be patient and wait for him to lead. Because his parents never wanted to let him go, it became natural for him to react like a child when there was any conflict; this did not suit his wife who had been used to having to fight for survival, and who liked disagreements to be aired and argued out.

The emotional scars of her childhood had left Penny with an abysmally low self-image, and she was always ready to assume that she was no good and that people didn't like her. Bob had to learn to understand this and to be supportive when things upset her.

Besides influences left by parents and upbringing, your reactions may also be determined by your place in the family. In *Your Place in the Family*, Barbara Sullivan has written at length on this subject from a Christian viewpoint. The book is well worth reading in order to discover how your union as a married couple may be affected by early relationships with siblings. There is certainly no suggestion that a couple need to have a similar background in order for the marriage to work; it is a question of understanding what kind of people the experiences have made you and your partner into.

Visiting

The only child is at a particular disadvantage when it comes to giving time to parents, because obviously the more children the older couple have, the more widely will be spread the responsibility for visiting and entertaining them. This applies not only when they are old and need help looking after themselves, but also when they are younger and expect their newly married son or daughter to continue to visit them frequently. Steve was an only child whose mother was jealous of anyone else taking him over and expected to see him and his wife Lesley most weekends. He wasn't very close to his parents but was easy-going and complied with their wishes, until he and Lesley found that with two small children the frequent weekend visits were too much. Unfortunately his mother resented this. Things were also difficult because Steve's parents were not Christians and didn't understand the commitments that he and Lesley had on Sundays. However, when the parents started to go to church things improved, and they were able to agree on a more reasonable schedule of visiting.

It's a good idea, during a visit to or from the in-laws, to spend time with them – perhaps having a meal out together – without children or other members of the family. This is particularly beneficial if the children tend to act as a catalyst for discord. On the other hand, if the recipe for disaster in your family is for the two couples to be alone together, then this plan is obviously better avoided. Some people complain that their in-laws take no interest in them or the grand-children, while others find that the problem is that they come for a visit and outstay their welcome. This is, of course, only likely to happen when the older couple are not working, and may also arise more often if the parent lives alone. You may feel less able to suggest that they go home if you know that loneliness is in store for them.

It is a pity that those who are guilty of extended visits cannot realise that if they stayed for briefer periods they would probably be asked back more often. It is essential that the husband and wife are honest with each other about this sort of situation, and try to explain how they feel without causing offence. For example, a husband might say, 'I really would prefer your mother not to come while you're in hospital – we don't seem to get on very well when you're not here. I'll take time off work when you go in, and we'll invite your mother to help you when you come out.'

When a social visit is arranged it is not sensible for it to be open-ended. A wife could say, 'Last time when your parents stayed for three weeks I did find it very tiring. Let's invite them for a week this time, and you can drive them home and visit your sister. Then we'll ask them for another week in the summer and they can come for Annie's birthday.' Once you have agreed on how the invitation should be worded, you can put it to the in-laws as coming from both of you.

Christmas is a traditional time for families to get together, but unfortunately it is also a time when there is a high rate of marriage breakdown (as well as of suicide among lonely people). As we shall see later on with holidays, Christmas can be a time of strain because you will both want to make the most of your time at home but may have different ideas about how to do this; if there are children, the situation can become still more tense. You will probably feel that you must either visit or invite your parents to stay at Christmas, especially if you have a widowed parent dependent on you alone for visits. If you don't get on together, or the hostess is constantly working single-handed in the kitchen, the season of goodwill feels like an endurance test. Threatened with a Christmas like this, you are fortunate if you live close enough to make day trips instead. Most young married couples (with or without children) would probably agree that it is nice to have some Christmases at home without guests, and if you want to do this, you should take advantage of the years when your parents are not old and alone.

Needing privacy?
It is not only at Christmas that tension can be caused by the presence of visitors. Some couples find that their marriage

doesn't function well with other people around, whether they are family members or not. If you are among those who need to clear the air with heated arguments you will be inhibited from doing this because it would be rude and embarrassing in front of other people. Moreover, certain guests can even seem to act as a catalyst for marital discord by sparking off an adverse reaction in one partner. On the other hand, there is also a danger for couples who are very hospitable and keep open house but find it hard to talk to each other, because they may be sheltering behind the presence of visitors in order to avoid communicating at a deep level.

It may seem selfish to make so much of the need for a couple to be alone together, but if this is important in your marriage it is foolish to ignore it, and you should certainly think and pray long and hard *together* before inviting any long-term guests into your home. This becomes particularly relevant if you face the question of an elderly parent coming to live with you; a lonely person's problems are not always best solved in this way, and it is often preferable to help them to move into some self-contained accommodation close to your home. If elderly parents get past the stage at which they can look after themselves, even in a 'granny flat', their children may find they are under considerable pressure from society to take them in and nurse them. This can be disastrous to a marriage, because it may cause feelings of guilt and resentment, and will almost certainly make the carers so exhausted that they have little time to spare for each other.

If it is possible for the patient to have twenty-four-hour care by trained people in a pleasant nursing home this can be better for all concerned.

To quote Selwyn Hughes again, he says that though it is not always possible to make rules about relations with in-laws (and others), the rule that a marriage ought to be protected should be made and kept, because creation orders it. A married person should therefore never ignore their partner's views on extending hospitality and sharing their home, and the effect on any children they may have should not be ignored either.

Questions to ask

Would it help you to tolerate your in-laws' views and criticisms if you tried to imagine yourself in their position?

Do you still allow your parents to influence your thinking and your actions more than is appropriate now that you are married?

Do you preserve a balance between being hospitable to your in-laws and friends, and preserving privacy for your family?

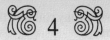

4

The Patter of Muddy Wellies

Many couples underestimate the enormous, and sometimes traumatic, change that parenthood can have on their relationship. If they know it exists in some families they assume that as Christians they will be immune. We need to be realistic and acknowledge that, although children are a gift and a blessing from God, they can be an extra source of tension. If there are already worries over housing, health or employment, children can strain relations to breaking point. The NSPCC, who are called to around a hundred cases of child abuse every day, report that in at least half of these there are problems within the marriage.

Learning to adapt
Most of us who are parents – Christian or otherwise – will feel very guilty if we reach the point of even being tempted to harm our child, and yet it is easy to be driven to this state by a baby who won't sleep or a toddler who grizzles all the time. Feelings of guilt when we can't cope, disappointment when the excitement of parenthood wears off, frustration at not having enough time to be ourselves, can cause unexpected tensions in the marriage, and this makes us more on edge and less able to cope with a fractious child. Even couples who have waited many years, and longed and prayed for a child, can be disillusioned when parenthood becomes a reality, perhaps because they have so glamourised the idea that they are blind to any drawbacks, and possibly because without realising it they have become very used to there being only two of them.

Terry and Louise were such a couple, who were blessed – after many years of disappointment – with a little boy who screamed all the time. They found that the strain the baby put on their marriage was just as great as the strain of childlessness. Louise found it difficult to get used to the idea of having just a baby to talk to all day after being for so long in an interesting job, and Terry had to adapt to the fact that at weekends he was no longer free to do as he liked because Louise needed a break from the baby.

Another couple who came late to parenthood adopted a school-age child. This did not pose the same need to adapt, as the wife was able to continue her part-time job, but they did admit that it was a shock to find that they could no longer spend evenings in the same way – for example attending church together and then going on to a friend's house.

Holidays brought further need to adapt for Terry and Louise. They could no longer eat and sleep when they liked, visit all the places that interested them, and choose whether to climb a mountain or lie on the beach and read! Over the years, they had become so used to this kind of break that when they went away with the baby and were forced to give his needs priority, they didn't feel they had had a holiday at all.

It has been shown that, together with Christmas, holidays are a time when many marriages break up. Because the days are usually very limited and therefore precious, we naturally want to spend as much time as possible doing the things we enjoy. But children have their own ideas of what constitutes a good day out, and all this can cause conflict between the parents who are responsible for deciding what to do. It is a clever family that can juggle their time and activities so that everyone is satisfied, and a fortunate one that can find a holiday location that is the heart's desire of parents and children alike.

The problems of adapting to children in everyday life are by no means confined to new parents – as we shall see, the strain is likely to increase as the children get older; nor do the difficulties hit only couples who have become set in their ways. On the contrary, having children too early in a marriage can lead to disaster. Two divorced women whom I spoke to recently had both suffered from marrying young and having three children in quick succession. If you wait until you have grown used to each other (and have adequate housing) you may be more likely to cope with the advent of a new member of the family, and planning the age gaps between children can mean that you won't feel over-whelmed by a houseful of little ones all at once.

To be or not to be

There is obviously no one right time to start a family and each Christian couple should be guided by what they believe is God's will. In society generally, there seems to be a tendency – for various reasons – to delay having the first child for several years; but in Christian circles there can be a strong feeling that children follow automatically after marriage. In some churches a woman who chooses to have a career instead of a family is frowned upon, even though she may have made this decision because she knows she wouldn't be happy at home, and wouldn't want to give the care of the child to someone else.

There are Christians who feel that all forms of contraception are wrong and others who feel that marriage is for 'mutual comfort and the procreation of children'. It is probably true that God does want most Christian couples to have children, because that is how he made them, although some are infertile and have no 'miracle' baby. However, if you don't have children you are more flexible, more free to travel and able to give more of your time and energy to working for the Lord – and a single person is even more free (1 Corinthians 7.32–34). A missionary couple, for example, would have fewer problems if they had no dependent children, and many have to decide that they must return home because of their children's education. God can certainly make great use of childless couples, whether they are childless by choice or not, and may well

42

want some others to wait a few years before starting a family.

As Christians you should therefore not feel browbeaten into having children before it is right, and should consider all the practical points as you seek God's guidance. This may mean that you will have to ignore pressure which – sadly – often comes from within the church. Alan and Julia were very active for the Lord both in their secular jobs in the local hospital and in their church. Knowing that this involvement would have to lessen if they had children, they decided to wait a few years. One day some people from another fellowship came and asked if they could pray together, as they had a message for them from the Lord. Alan and Julia were surprised to find that this was a word of encouragment, and that they would have a child. The messengers were quite put out to learn that Julia was not having trouble conceiving and that they weren't even trying for a baby! Fortunately Alan and Julia were not upset by this and continued to do what they felt God wanted; possibly the message was entirely false, or maybe it was intended to be an encouragement to them in the future if parenthood did not come when they wanted it.

It is, of course, foolish to enter marriage without agreeing on whether you want one or more children, or none; who would stay at home with them; and what to do about contraception. Some Christians don't decide about contraception until it is too late and start a family by default. The question of birth control will not be dealt with in any detail since there is a book on the subject in the *Christian Woman* series. There are Christians who believe that they should use no methods of birth control and allow God to give them the children he wants them to have. But there is no reason for God to override nature and, unless they have difficulty conceiving, they could end up with a dozen or more children. One alternative is to believe that as God has given us several acceptable types of contraception, we should use one until we feel him guiding us to have a child; but in this case it is important to remain open to his leading.

Adjusting your life-style

Although many middle-aged people now have the opportunity to attend pre-retirement courses to prepare for their drastic change in lifestyle, no such facility is available in the way of pre-parenthood classes. This is odd, because although leaving a job and being at home all day must come as a difficult adjustment to an active man or woman in their sixties, a young mother has to cope with this as well as the responsibility for the new baby and the effect parenthood will have on her marriage. The advice one receives at ante-natal classes may include things like, 'Watch out for signs of jealously if you ignore your husband in favour of the baby', or 'If you get lonely, join a mother and baby club'. But this is rather superficial and in any case if the baby is already on the way it is too late to warn a woman that she may not be ready for parenthood. Advice and counselling would be more useful before pregnancy, and if anyone is put off, then it is probably better if they don't embark on having a baby.

The reaction to this suggestion could be, 'What rubbish! I didn't need counselling – I just got on with it', or 'If God wants us to have children, he will provide the resources we need'. This may be the case for a Christian whose family life is a perfect reflection of the biblical pattern, but surely the high incidence of postnatal depression and loneliness – not to mention child abuse and broken marriages (even among Christians) – would indicate that a great deal of suffering could be alleviated if potential parents, particularly mothers, were more prepared for the change. If you are planning to give up work to have a baby, such classes could encourage you to make friends with mothers who are also at home with children, and to keep in touch with your ex-colleagues who could talk to you about work. You could think in advance about the benefit of having a couple of hobbies, and of getting out as much as possible, sometimes with the baby and sometimes without.

It's obviously with the first child that the problem of adjustment is most acute; although for a while the mother whose baby sleeps well may actually find she has more time for leisure activities or study at home than her friend who has to cope with a toddler as well.

If you have enjoyed your job – whether for companionship or intellectual satisfaction – you may feel the loss keenly when the excitement of pregnancy and birth has worn off. Your husband will need to understand this (which should be easy enough if he imagines having to give up his job) and make an effort to be a stimulating companion in the evenings, however tired he may feel. He must show you that he doesn't regard you as less of a person because you're not working, and should encourage you to take up interests and activities outside the home.

One problem which hits many marriages is that a young husband will often work long hours, either doing paid overtime to make up for his wife's loss of income, or doing the kind of unpaid overtime which the professional person hopes will lead to promotion. If you have been at home all day with a young baby, there is all the difference in the world between a husband who comes in at 5.30 and one who returns at 7.30. If your husband is willing to walk through the door and be interested in his baby while you escape to sort out the chaos in the kitchen, you will appreciate him much more than if he expects the child to be asleep and his meal on the table the minute he appears. The yearning for adult conversation and someone to hold the baby at busy moments increases rapidly throughout the day, which is why you may seem unreasonably angry if your husband is late home from work. From this point of view, I was better able to cope with my third child than my first, because although my husband still came in late, my long afternoon was broken up by the arrival home of my much older children.

Some women find the loneliness and isolation at home with a young baby so great that they decide to return to work, and there can then be problems if the husband is not happy for the baby to be consigned to a creche or childminder. Of course, if you do not intend to stay at home for

45

more than a few months, you and your husband need to talk about this before you start your family and perhaps consider whether it is right to have children at all – or perhaps whether your husband wants to look after the little one instead. On the other hand, you may have always intended to care for your child at home, but have found that you are becoming depressed and frustrated and are taking it out on your husband or child. If you had been able to foresee this before the pregnancy, perhaps your husband could have modified his hours or you could have tried to develop some job or hobby that you could do at home. Failing this, it may be better for you to take a part-time job rather than to risk spoiling the chance of relating well to your husband or child.

People in the churches – and the community as a whole – need to be more aware of the loneliness of young mothers, especially the ones who have recently moved house or who have no transport, and before we criticise those who return to work we should ask ourselves what effort we have made to lessen their problems.

Planning your policies
Another thing which you need to talk through in advance is what general principles will govern the upbringing of any children you may have.

There are two extreme attitudes to child-rearing, both of which can be equally damaging either to the child or the marriage. One is the self-orientated approach – I want children, but I don't intend to give up my job, or alter my social life. This can be damaging to the child, who becomes just an appendage instead of an integral part of the family. The other extreme is the child-orientated attitude, which causes one or both parents (more often the mother) to centre their lives so much on the child's needs that they have no time for each other, let alone outside activities, so the marriage is likely to suffer.

I once heard a joke about a couple who started off with six theories on child-rearing and no children, and ended up with six children and no theories! My point, however, is not that we should have a theory for handling any problem that may arise, just that we should know in advance what sort of standards we are going to set for our family. These can vary greatly even among Christians, some of whom are such gentle, loving people that they are often too lenient with their children, while others go overboard for the 'spare the rod and spoil the child' philosophy. There are those who feel that children should be taught from an early age to sit through church services, while others think this is quite wrong and like their youngsters to go to a class appropriate for their age; others believe that as they get older children shouldn't be forced to go to church at all. Then there is the question of eating habits – whether, for example, the children are to be allowed to indulge in sweets or whether a rigid programme of 'healthy eating' is to be enforced.

The question of the parents getting out alone together is one which also needs to be considered. One of you may imagine that you will join a babysitting circle like most of your friends, but the other may only be willing to leave the children with your mother who lives ten miles away and cannot drive. Certainly some people do prefer to have relations or very close friends babysitting, and some mothers will not leave a baby at all until it is fully weaned. I recently encountered an extreme case of a couple who had made the decision never to leave their children with any babysitter, either in the daytime or the evening. They had therefore not been out alone together for some five years and had many more similar years to come. Such a policy is so potentially stunting to a marriage that it is difficult to see how it could be justified, and both partners would need to be wholeheartedly committed to it.

Another situation that seems to arise in 'child-orientated' marriages is that of 'musical beds'. The wakeful baby is sometimes fed in bed and he and the mother may drop off together. Then the small child starts to come into his parents' bed for comfort, maybe just in the early morning but often if he wakes in the night as well. As he gets bigger it becomes a squash in the four feet six inches bed, so one of the parents is exiled to the child's room. Some parents tolerate 'musical beds', others actually encourage it (and regard those who don't as peculiar!), while many reluctantly accept the fact that they will be woken by a bouncing child rather than an alarm clock in the morning. When this happens, the parents' bed is no longer their own private haven, and this can play havoc with their sex life, not to mention prayer times and a good night's rest. If you are not in absolute agreement about your policy on bed-sharing there maybe tension and jealousy. I believe that here the interests of safeguarding the marriage should come before the (supposed) interests of the child.

Many of these matters are purely personal, and you shouldn't be criticised for the stand you have chosen, but it is important that you both agree on the rules or guidelines and back each other up. Most people would agree that it is very bad to argue about such things in front of the children, and a child who senses the disagreement will often try to play one parent off against the other. However, if your marriage is going through a bad patch and you are constantly bickering, it is very difficult to present a united front to the children, especially if you genuinely disagree on the issue under discussion. Even if no argument has taken place in front of them, the children may still be the cause of another row if one parent feels that the other is always taking the child's part. Such situations are unlikely to improve until the marriage as a whole is repaired.

Jealousy

Jealousy of one's own children is usually associated with a young father who finds his wife so taken up with the baby that he feels left out. The meal you used to share together is interrupted by the baby crying for a feed or not wanting to settle, lovemaking is disturbed at just the wrong moment because the baby needs attention, or perhaps you're just too exhausted. You may find it difficult to concentrate on anything other than the baby so that conversation becomes stunted, or feel depressed and take it out on your partner.

The new father will find it helps if he gets involved in the care of the baby and the jobs around the house. This is not just a cosmetic involvement to make him feel wanted, as one might ask a toddler to go and fetch a clean nappy for the baby and then praise him to make him feel grown-up and helpful. With the father it is the beginning of a relationship with his baby which can perhaps become as deep as the one you have. He has some ground to catch up on, since the baby was growing for nine months inside you while he could only feel the kicks from the outside, but it is sad if he feels he can't do much for his child until he can read to it or teach it to play football.

A father who becomes as involved as time will allow with all aspects of his baby's care will be able to share your wonder and excitement at the beautiful little person who has become part of your family, and you will get added pleasure from seeing him relate to the baby. In addition to this, the more helpful he can be to you in practical ways, the more time and energy you will be able to devote to him and to looking after yourself. He should try to understand the physical and emotional changes that have taken place in you, and you should make sure you show him that he is no less important to you than he was before.

Jealousy, however, is not confined to fathers and young babies and can often arise when the children are older. A young child who has just learned to talk will try to monop-olise any conversation, and it is very important for you both to be able to talk to each other in spite of your children. A husband who has waited all day to tell you something will be understandably resentful if you allow yourself to be distracted every time the child demands attention. It is even worse if your husband ignores you when you have already had to tolerate the child's ceaseless chatter all day. Of course the answer could be to put the children to bed early and then sit down and talk, but this is easier said than done, especially if one of you has to go out during the evening.

Some fathers actually find excuses not to go home until the children are safely in bed, but the more human face of fatherhood is shown in men like Trevor, who liked to play with his children when he got in. His wife Sally, having coped with a large family all day, was eager to spend some time peacefully with him, and often wished he would not keep the children up. You can easily feel guilty if you are jealous of the time your husband invests with the children, but it is very difficult if you feel that your emotional needs are not being met because you are not able to spend enough time with him. If it is right for you to have children, it must be possible to divide the time up and still have some left for each other, but this may mean that some other commitment will have to be sacrificed, as we shall see in the next chapter.

The marriage will also be under strain if you relate better to one child and your partner to another. The battles of authority result in your blaming each other for being too strict or too lenient and being inconsistent in the treatment of the two children. This problem can especially arise if the children are of different sexes. Even greater problems occur, of course, when a parent tries to relate to step-children and to treat them in the same way as the natural children. The step-parent may feel that perfectly normal problems were caused only by the fact that he or she is a substitute parent.

The afterthought

Possibly the most difficult adjustment for parents to make is when they are faced with the arrival of an unplanned baby, especially if it is at a time when they feel their family has been complete for many years. I have encountered a surprising number of such pregnancies among Christians – in fact a few years ago more than half of my friends who were pregnant were in that state unintentionally! I did wonder whether God wanted his people to have larger families, or whether non-Christians were having unwanted pregnancies as well but were choosing to have abortions. This is, of course, a temptation which Christians today are faced with, especially if they are quite old and are warned that the baby might be handicapped.

If you feel that you have made a responsible decision, under God, to limit your family, it is not surprising that shock and resentment should be the initial reaction to an unexpected pregnancy, and Christians are not immune to this. However, fortunately, as the months go by, most couples seem able to accept that the new baby is part of God's plan for their lives. Some, like Linda, who had two children and definitely didn't want a third, suffer depression throughout the pregnancy but feel much happier once the baby has been born. To those who are very unhappy about it, it could obviously cause problems in the marriage relationship, particularly if one partner blithely accepts it as God's will and expects the other to do so just as easily.

Roger and Brenda were in their forties and believed that their family of three children, ranging from eight to fourteen, was complete, when they realised with a shock that Brenda was pregnant again. After many years of using no contraception, they had just started to do so, and this made it easier for them to accept that God must have wanted them to have the baby. Yet even as they surrendered to his will they admitted that it wasn't what they would have chosen. Roger realised that it was harder for Brenda because her life would be the most affected. He insisted that she keep her part-time job open, feeling that if she didn't get over her resentment it would be better for everyone if she went back to work. As it turned out, Brenda was glad to have a break from her job and found it a pleasant change to be at home with the baby and to have time to herself when he was asleep. She and Roger are a spiritually mature couple with a secure marriage which survived this upheaval; they actually felt that it benefited the family, as the arrival of the baby drew the older children closer to them, and made them realise how easily an accidental pregnancy can happen.

Not as easy as it sounds

For those who are infertile or who frequently miscarry, any talk of contraception and unplanned pregnancies must sound like a sick joke. Many childless wives say what pangs of longing and envy they feel when they see small babies or expectant mothers, and some women pregnant for the third or fourth time are reticent about sharing the news with their less fortunate friends.

To some people their infertility is a dawning realisation as the months and years go by and nothing happens; to others it is a sudden shock when they see the results of tests. There are a few couples who go into marriage knowing that one of them has a medical history that will make it impossible for them to have a child. Such marriages must have a stronger foundation than most, because a person who wants children would have to love his or her partner very much indeed to marry them knowing that parenthood was impossible.

Neil and Geraldine married knowing that Neil could not father children. He was offered a slim hope if he had a major operation, but they decided that it was not worth the risk. They had already agreed to adopt, but did not rush into it, as Geraldine did not have a strong maternal instinct. She considered adoption a relatively easy way of becoming a mother as she had always been scared of giving birth. This does not seem to be a common view, however, and many find the adoption procedure, the waiting and the disappointments, very traumatic. Neil and Geraldine had the advantage that they had never considered anything else, so they didn't have to change from hoping for a child of their own to considering adoption.

One question which did arise with Neil and Geraldine, however, as with many other couples where the husband is infertile, is that of artificial insemination by donor. This can be a real temptation to a woman who longs to bear a child herself. In the converse situation, where the wife is infertile, some have sought to employ a surrogate mother. Another option now available is the 'test-tube' baby. All these

unnatural methods have different moral and ethical implications which each Christian couple has to decide and pray
about for themselves. The secular attitude is that everyone
has the right to have a child no matter how it is produced,
and as Christians we need to know why we disagree (if we
do). Once again, a large problem occurs if the two partners
find they are not in agreement about what is an acceptable
way to deal with their situation.

Many childless couples must get tired of hearing stories
about 'miracle' babies born to people who thought they
were infertile, and we have to be aware of the fact that God
by no means always moves in this way. However, I include
the following story because what happened enabled the
couple to learn about their motives for wanting to be
parents. Robert and Hilary had been trying for a baby for
many years and Hilary had taken fertility drugs, sometimes
with unpleasant results but never with success. They were
beginning to feel resentful and couldn't help being envious
of the many people they knew who were producing babies
with no problem. Believing that God wanted them to have
a child, they prayed about it, and when they decided to
apply for adoption they were accepted very quickly. Soon
after this, Hilary became pregnant, but she said they would
always value the way the adoption application had forced
them to take stock and actually put into words why they
wanted to have a child. To begin with they had simply felt
that it was the next step in their marriage, but as time went
by it became a desperate need, and they both felt able to
love and accept any child God gave them, whether through
adoption or naturally. Most of us do not think of assessing
our reasons for wanting children, but perhaps if more
potential parents did it there would not be so many who
started producing children simply because it seemed to be
'the thing to do'.

John and I did not analyse our reasons for wanting our
first two children because that was something we felt totally
committed to, but when we started thinking about having
a third there was a great deal of heart-searching. At one

stage I remember making a list of 'fors and againsts', but as John was not sufficiently in favour at that time, and doubted if he could feel the same about a third child as he did about the other two, the idea was dropped. A few years later we had detailed discussions about the idea of having two more children, and this time we both felt sure it was right. Even so, we didn't foresee the much greater strain that this would put on the family in terms of increasing commitments and the need to reorganise priorities.

Questions to ask

Why do you really want to become a parent/have more children?

In what ways will you have to alter your lifestyle if you do?

What adverse effects could parenthood have on your marriage relationship? How will you deal with these?

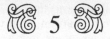

I Can't Be in Two Places at Once!

Your wedding anniversary falls on the evening you run the Girls' Brigade. Your boss wants you to do regular overtime on the same evening as your church's weekly Bible study. A weekend rally to which your young people's group is going clashes with your child's birthday. The job you would most like to do at church falls vacant just when you are busiest at home and at work. You are both expected to go to a business dinner on the night your child is in the school play. Most poignantly – a situation which nearly applied in our family – you are a husband called to your dying mother while your wife is giving birth. In all cases you are torn in half; you wish you could be in two places at once, or even three or four.

Sometimes the pressure comes from the fact that two events clash or it may be caused simply because there are not enough hours in the day to fit in all the calls on your time. Perhaps one particular decision has to be made, for example, changing jobs, moving house, taking on a new area of service, which will profoundly affect the other aspects of your life. In these situations you will have to decide where your priorities lie, and although every case has to be considered separately it is a help to have basic principles to work on.

A married person obviously has more problems in this area than a single one, and a married couple with children will find the decisions even more difficult. As a Christian couple (especially if you have children), you are potentially far more likely to be torn in two than your non-Christian neighbours. The calls on your time and attention are likely to be each other, your children, your wider families, your work, church activities, your involvement with helping other people, your personal spiritual life, and – dare I mention it? – your personal social life. I really believe that the inability to agree on priorities is a major cause of failure, or at least threatened failure, in Christian marriages.

Busy for the Lord?
The lives of many married Christians become complicated and pressurised because they feel they have to do so much: time must be spent alone with God, and more time is taken up worshipping at church and doing jobs in the church, as well as trying to evangelise and counsel friends and neighbours. Pressures over worship are reduced if the family are able to attend services together on Sundays; and if babysitting is a problem in the evenings, you can take turns. By far the greatest cause of pressure is overactivity in the fellowship. This can arise in either of two ways: your church may be the kind that gives an infinite number of jobs to anyone who shows themselves capable, or you may feel you must work in order to please God. If the two combine, the chances of a breakdown – either nervous or marital – must grow very high, but even if the situation is not so drastic, the problem needs to be dealt with.

Selwyn Hughes, speaking at a convention I attended, talked of the large number of people who have problems because they feel God is only pleased if they are working themselves into the ground for him. He quoted the following rhyme:

> Mary had a little lamb, 'twas given her to keep;
> But then it joined a Baptist church and died from lack
> of sleep!

I go to a Baptist church and I know the feeling, but judging from the response from the interdenominational audience it is common everywhere. It is something which we all need to sort out for ourselves, but if you are married you should be aware that your busy-ness is also having an adverse effect on your partner.

We should remember that many Christians are involved in the Lord's work in a wider sense and in a way not directly connected with their fellowship. They may be representatives for a Christian charity, or do voluntary work in a Christian bookshop or children's home. Some might be involved in interdenominational activities such as Mission England, and others might spend a lot of time on personal evangelism in their own neighbourhood. All these things will take time away from the family, and if you feel it is right to be busy in this way it may well not be appropriate for you also to have a job in the church.

Another drain on people's time is structural work in their church. For many wives it can be the last straw when a husband who is already busy at work and heavily involved in jobs within the fellowship goes off on a Saturday to paint the church hall. I recently met a vicar who will only have work done on the building if the church can afford to pay for it, because he feels it is wrong to take more time away from the people who are already doing Christian work which can't be delegated to contractors.

Setting aside the structural jobs, many churches are at fault because they allow a handful of people to be burdened with the lion's share of the church work. This is more understandable in small fellowships but it also happens in larger congregations. If someone is seen to do one job well they are automatically given the next one that becomes vacant. Of course, the obvious answer would be to say no, but some people are too polite – or too proud – to do this. Others may fall prey to the suggestion, 'If the Lord put it into the Rev X's heart to ask me, then it must be right for me to do it'. They forget that the Rev X is human and overworked like the rest of us and knows that if no one will take on the work he will probably have to do it himself. Moreover, he may be tempted to offer a job to the busy person he knows is immediately capable of it, rather than to the retiring introvert who needs to be drawn out and convinced of his own abilities.

The trouble comes in a marriage, not only if so many commitments are taken on that time for the family suffers, but also if the partners do not agree that the job is right. Probably you do always consult each other before taking on anything, but the one who objects to the new commitment can be made to feel guilty: why are they not willing for their partner to do this important work for the Lord? Diana Peck, writing in *There's Somebody at the Door*, relates that she once mentioned to a visiting missionary that she resented her husband spending so many evenings doing youth work, and she was told to 'take it to the cross'. If that advice was meant to mean that she should put up with it, then I would disagree. By choosing to marry and have children, her husband had taken on responsibilities to his family which couldn't be cancelled out by his involvement with the youth work.

Is the Church to blame?
It is better to attempt dissuasion, as forcefully as seems necessary, than to acquiesce reluctantly and then live to regret it. John and I spent a most miserable year when he was church treasurer. The job was such a tremendous burden to us as a family that I had to make a very great effort if I was to avoid grumbling about it, and I usually failed. My resentment was due partly to the fact that I had no idea of the extent of the job when he took it on, partly that he was often doing treasurer's work in the evenings and then staying up very late to complete other jobs, and partly because people seemed to assume that I was involved in the work as well and asked me questions that I knew nothing about.

Looking back, although I am not proud of the fact that I was constantly complaining and begging him to give up, I do feel that it was wrong for him to do it in the first place. Humanly speaking, he could not have been more suited to the post and he made a better job of it than most people in the church could have done, but that doesn't necessarily mean that it was what God wanted at the time. I later discovered that a previous treasurer had also suffered many marital arguments because of his duties in that job. In his case, it was not that his wife objected to his being busy, for he later took on an even more onerous position – she just felt the job of treasurer was wrong. To him it had seemed the obvious thing to do – again because it fitted in with his natural abilities – but he now acknowledges that he went into it wrongly, without seeking the Lord's guidance.

New Christians are particularly vulnerable in this area, for several reasons. First, they will feel that it must be 'Christian' to say yes. Secondly, they will have less idea of the pressures a job may bring. Thirdly, they probably need to concentrate on the new dimension in their marriage rather than becoming so busy that they see much less of each other.

Andrew and Fiona became Christians together and were given a warm welcome into their church. Because they were generous, outgoing people they were soon asked to help with this and that, until within a couple of years of being confirmed they had a Bible study in their home, Fiona was a Sunday school teacher, a church visitor and a member of the tea committee, while Andrew was a youth leader and a member of both the evangelism group and the parochial church council.

Although Andrew and Fiona didn't make any attempt to turn down these jobs, the church was still at fault for offering them without thinking about the amount of time that was suddenly being taken away from them as a family. Nevertheless, they survived, although they had no time for growing together as a Christian couple and were constantly torn between church duties and their three teenagers, who weren't Christians. Then the crunch came: Andrew, though still a 'baby' Christian, was elected churchwarden – a job to which he was quite unsuited and which Fiona felt sure he shouldn't do. It was not just the time factor and the responsibility which caused them problems; they also discovered for the first time that these lovely Christian people were constantly complaining about the most petty oversights or mistakes in the job he was struggling to do.

The stress that Andrew was under at church caused a great deal of tension in his marriage and resulted in frequent rows. Fiona often stayed away from church because she didn't feel she could worship when she wasn't right with Andrew, and when she did go, and managed to achieve a mood of praise, it was inevitably spoilt by the people who came to grumble at Andrew in his position as churchwarden. They gave up their other commitments, but it was too late to start again. They felt disillusioned with the church which had appeared to welcome them but had then used them, and they couldn't understand why their marriage was less happy than it had been before they became Christians.

To be fair to the church, Andrew and Fiona were no doubt given jobs to help them feel at home and to show them they were needed. Far more caution should be used over this, and particularly if one partner is not a Christian, any job offered should one which will have the least effect on the home life. If both you and your husband have recently become Christians, it would be a good idea for you to sit down together with your minister or a church leader and discuss which single job you would each feel happy to do in the church, maybe separately, maybe together. The church should be aware, however, that even if one person takes on a job, the partner is bound to be affected by it – taking phone calls, carrying messages, helping the other to remember things, and calming them down if they get nervous about it.

Work versus home life

These points about involving the other partner will also apply, of course, to secular work or to study. Sometimes you will continue your education after marriage, perhaps by attending evening classes, doing an Open University or correspondence course, or by completing a higher degree. If you do this in the daytime while caring for young children it may not cause many problems, but if one of you is working full-time and studying in the evening, it can put a great strain on the relationship, especially if there are children around. I have known people who have felt that the PhD was the greatest potential marriage-breaker. One woman said that the most difficult period was when her husband took time off work to complete his studies in the daytime and she had to keep the children away from him.

A man or woman who works from home or who receives frequent phone messages at home should be sensitive to the effect this may have on the partner. With the obvious exception of doctors and others who are on call for emergencies, Christians should make it plain to their colleagues or customers that they do not expect phone calls on a Sunday. It is also good to try to be firm about not taking calls during mealtimes and not talking on the phone at length when other family activities are being disturbed. This, of course, applies to social phone calls as well as business ones, but somehow the latter are worse. There is nothing more frustrating for a wife whose husband arrives home late and finally sits down to the meal she has prepared, than for him to be immediately summoned to the phone by the very work he has only just left. While considering how this aspect of life affects us and our families it is worth sparing a thought for our vicar or pastor who, unless he is a Catholic, is very likely to be married. His wife and children are not angels, any more than he is, and may well feel resentment if he is constantly disturbed at mealtimes, bedtime, or on his day off. Clergy marriages seem to be going through a rough time these days, and we can do our bit to help by respecting the fact that the minister's need for privacy and normal family life is the same as ours.

All this, of course, calls into question our whole attitude to work. A Christian will obviously be conscientious and want to give of his (or her) best, which means that he may work harder than some of his colleagues, but on the other hand – since money is not his god – he will not be obsessed with the need to work overtime to get even more of it. The single person is free to throw himself into his work and may be wise to do so if his home life seems lonely or empty. When you are married, however, your job must not prevent you from spending an appropriate amount of time with your family.

The word 'appropriate' must be subjective, since what suits one couple will not suit another, and it will also depend on whether you have children, and if so how many. A childless couple *may* take a conscious decision to devote a vast amount of time to their jobs and rarely see each other, though this is not recommended, but young children cannot be treated in the same way, and need a lot of their parents' time and attention. It is also important, if a baby is on the way, for a husband to realise that his wife's need of him is going to increase greatly around the time of the birth, and he should do as much as possible to free himself from work commitments which involve a lot of overtime or travelling far away from home.

It is essential that the lines of communication remain open, so that if you or your partner feels neglected you can explain how you are reacting. It may be tempting to broach this subject when the workaholic husband or wife stumbles over the threshold two hours late, but that is obviously not sensible. If you are greeted with constant grumbling, however justified, on your return from work you are not likely to want to come home earlier the next day, even if your conscience tells you that you should. As with all other problems that need to be discussed, it is a good idea to sit down to a tête-à-tête supper with the phone off the hook and the children in bed, or even to go out somewhere and talk in a change of scene. If the whole problem is that you never get a chance to see each other, you will have to make a determined effort to break out of the vicious circle.

Promotion can bring problems, particularly if it involves moving to another part of the country. It may seem quite normal to some people for the man's job to assume such importance that the whole family is uprooted every few years. But unless the move is made for the benefit of the wife's career as well, it will almost certainly be harder for her to settle in the new neighbourhood, whether she is missing her previous job and having to look for a new one, or whether she is at home with young children and feeling lonely. Christian couples ought to think and pray seriously about changing jobs and moving, and not simply assume that a better job must be right. Another area where sensitivity is needed is when a Christian feels led to leave the security of a job which has a 'tied' house; it may be very difficult for his wife to accept the possibility of homelessness.

Problems often arise because some men believe that they are indispensable to their work. This is rarely true, but the feeling may be caused by the fact that they are not sufficiently involved at home and have to feel needed somewhere. It results in the husband being unable to draw the line when meetings or phone calls threaten to interrupt family activities, and being unwilling to take sick leave or holidays. This can occur not just with the professional or high-powered businessman, but also with the one who is struggling to run his own shop or to survive as a self-employed craftsman. If your overworked husband does agree to take a week or a fortnight's break, he will probably work twice as hard in the days leading up to it, so that you will have to make all the holiday preparations yourself, and by the time you do get away you will both be completely exhausted. This may be another reason for holidays being a time of stress rather than relaxation. It will be made worse if your husband resents the fact that he has been persuaded to go away and worries all the time about the work he should be doing.

Jealousy again

Although it is more often the husband who has this over-commitment to his job, it can happen the other way round, as in the case of Shirley, who was entitled to six weeks' holiday but took only a few days because of staffing problems in her office. Her husband Sam resented this, especially as it meant that their children were left alone for long periods during the school holidays. He had just started a new job and wasn't able to take time off to be with the children, but he did feel that the family should come first, and he was more willing than Shirley to adapt his working hours and limit his commitment in order to devote time to the family.

Probably Sam was also jealous of Shirley's involvement with her work; certainly, many women find that they are jealous of their husband's work. It can happen if you have been unable to find a satisfactory job or have given up work to have children and then see your husband becoming more and more immersed in his career. Jealousy is an unpleasant word and one that Christians may prefer to hide from. It is so often linked with sexual activity that you may feel you are accusing your husband of a guilty relationship with his secretary if you admit to being jealous. However, what you envy is far more likely to be the intellectual relationship he has with his colleagues, coupled with the fact that he has an interesting job and is surrounded by stimulating company.

If you are the partner who is enjoying job satisfaction and your other half is either at home all day or putting up with uncongenial work, it is important to be sensitive to the way they feel, rather than criticising them for their 'un-Christian' attitutude. The best way to show your jealous partner that he (or she) is really important to you is by being sensitive to the life he is leading and the things which are lacking in it, and being willing to listen to his account of a boring day at home or at work. It is also helpful to show that colleagues at work are not as important to you as your family, and you can do this by not taking on extra commitments to them (like lifts home every evening) without considering how this will affect your own home life.

It is also difficult when customers, clients, patients, etc., claim a person's time outside working hours. The neglected wife or husband may feel jealous and wonder why other people's demands are more important than the family's, whereas the partner will simply see it as the conscientious carrying out of work or Christian service. In these circumstances, a spot of role-swapping can be very useful, as it was for us when I started to spend some Saturdays working in our Christian bookshop. I had never understood why John could not leave his office the minute it closed, regardless of what still needed to be done, but I soon found in the shop that a last-minute rush of customers or a problem with the cashing-up could easily keep me there for another half hour. He, on the other hand, discovered what it was like to be at home all day with young children, feeling that your partner is doing something more stimulating and wishing they would come home earlier!

Achieving a balance

We all have to maintain a balance between carrying out our secular jobs in a conscientious manner, and serving the Lord in the church, and devoting time to the family God has given us. In addition to that, however, we all need time to be alone together with our partner. The more we can get to like and appreciate the same things, the more we shall be able to be together, because certain leisure activities like swimming or watching football or going to a concert can be shared instead of indulged in separately. It is a good idea also to set aside time each week for just *being* together, in addition to any opportunities there may be of *doing* things or *going* to places together.

A few days after writing this, I happened to hear a talk by the wife of the director of the Operation Mobilisation ship *Doulos*. She told us that because her husband was so busy, she used to feel that she had to queue up with everyone else to see him, and they never had enough time together. She found it was even worse when she read books on this subject, because they always said (just as I am doing in this book!) that she needed to spend time alone with her husband, and it just wasn't possible. So she prayed that God would give them the time together that he knew they needed and not just what she wanted or other people advised.

This is obviously good advice, but I make no apology for

continuing to suggest that we try to make time for each other. We mustn't be put off by the fact that – as with the regular time we try to set aside for private prayer – something almost inevitably interrupts. A Sunday evening may suit some couples, because work will not intrude and it is not unreasonable to send the children to bed early, ready for school the next day. However, Sunday has its drawbacks because if one partner is delayed at the evening service or wants to call on a sick person on the way home, the other may resent this erosion of their time together. Also, if the time is used for talking over things that have been niggling during the week, an argument may result which will destroy the spirit of worship which has been achieved in the Sunday services and that will be a bad way to prepare for the dreaded Monday morning. The advantage of Sunday, on the other hand, is that if you are very busy with work and household jobs during the week but regard Sunday as a day of rest, you will at least be able to just sit down and be together without wanting to rush off and get things done.

It is a shame that we often feel guilty about our use of time, but it easily happens when time is at a premium and we know that wasted hours can never be regained. We need to decide what constitutes 'wasting' time. Certainly 'investing' it with our loved ones should not be regarded as wasteful, nor is it wrong to allow ourselves some time to use our God-given abilities. Sadly, many Christians seem to frown on activities such as sport, art classes, a drama group or a secular meeting, not because they are bad in themselves but because they are not as worthwhile as cleaning the church, preparing a Sunday school lesson, or going out evangelising. Christians should be good stewards of their time, as of their money, but God has not put us in this wonderful world to have all work and no play.

Whereas it is good for married people to have as much as possible in common, it is also necessary for each of us to have time to ourselves. Some people – particularly those women who tend to live life through their children – will need to make a conscious effort to give time to themselves.

But others who have a time-consuming sport or hobby (for example, cricket, which can take up a whole afternoon and evening at weekends as well as a midweek practice), may need to modify their activities for the sake of their marriage. You are fortunate if you recognise before you marry that your partner's hobby is a part of who he is, and accept it from the start, but this does not absolve him from being considerate in the way he goes about it.

When Suzanne married Ian she knew that music would always be his life even though he had not been able to make his career in it, and it was an interest that she shared. The fact that he was always keen to hurry home from work as early as possible to be with his family made up for the fact that many of his evenings were spent attending choir practices and giving clarinet lessons, and he always consulted her before booking up an evening. However, Ian had another interest – bird-watching – which took up a lot of his time, particularly in the holidays, and after they had children it was inevitable that Suzanne became excluded. She felt upset about this, partly because he seemed to need to be alone in this way and she felt left out, and partly because, though money was tight he spent a great deal on his bird-watching holidays. These are the kind of tensions that need to be talked out.

Another thing which can assume an unwarranted priority in some marriages is commitment to the home in the sense of the building we live in. Some women are so house-proud that not only do they cause tension by expecting the family to live in a museum rather than a home, but they also spend an unnecessary amount of time in house-work instead of with their husbands, children or friends. The male version of this 'house worshipping' phenomenon is the man who becomes obsessed with the idea of do-it-yourself home improvements. Obviously it is easy for his wife to become jealous of the time he is spending on this work instead of being with her; or it may be that she wants him to finish a job, but he realises that he has taken on too much and finds excuses to be away from the home instead. Either or both partners can also fall into the trap of finding 'essential' jobs to do in the house on a Sunday or other times which conflict with church activities, so that their spiritual lives suffer.

Adapting priorities

In many marriages the problem of dividing up one's time satisfactorily may never truly be solved, and it may be necessary to change the priorities as different circumstances intervene. One Christian wife, Sandra, told me that basically her priorities were to her husband first, her children next, then the church, followed by her secular job when she had one, and lastly her duties around the house; she also needed to make time to be alone. She felt that a couple who let church activities and their children take precedence over their marriage could be heading for danger, and she put the children before the church, because only she could be a mother to them, whereas several other people were capable of doing her Christian work.

During a period when her oldest child was doing 'A' levels and she had two much younger ones, Sandra and her husband decided not to go out together except when absolutely necessary because it wasn't fair to leave the teenager to look after his little sisters while he was so busy studying. Thus, for a limited period, the order of her priorities changed and she put the children before their marriage. But she and her husband knew that they must make a conscious effort to change back and do things together again as soon as they could.

Cliff and Karen were a busy couple who realised that their pace of life could only continue as it was while they remained childless; even so their commitments required quite a bit of juggling of time. They both taught in a boarding-school where they were houseparents. In addition to that, Cliff was doing a Bible correspondence course and had several positions of responsibility in the church. Although Karen enjoyed her job and therefore wasn't jealous of Cliff's, some of their friends were worried that

68

he was far too busy and that his church commitments made it impossible for him to spend any time with his wife.

However, Cliff and Karen had given the matter some thought and found that although in term-time they were ridiculously busy, in the long holidays they were able to make up for it. The fact that they lived and worked in the same place meant that they saw each other far more in the day than most couples do, and they were able to organise their timetables so that they had a half-day off together. They also drew the line at a commitment to the school which meant that Karen could hardly ever go out in the evening, and they insisted on a staffing arrangement that enabled them both to be off together. During term-time, if work and church clashed, they would give priority to work, but before they took on their jobs they had made sure that it would be possible for them to attend church regularly. Cliff and Karen's marriage survived because they were aware of the potential strains on it and had worked out ways of safeguarding their time together; they were also under no illusions that something would have to go if they became parents.

Questions to ask

What are your priorities regarding church, family, work, etc? Is your partner happy about this?

What is your real reason for agreeing to take on a job connected with the church?

If you have children, do they have any reason to resent your commitment to your job or to your church?

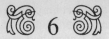

6

'When I Needed a Neighbour . . .'

Although it is always important for a husband and wife to devote time to each other, it is most necessary when things are going wrong. A twice-widowed Christian lady said that what she had gained from marriage was the knowledge that when trouble came she could allow herself to flow out to her husband and be warmed in the fire of his love. As the mother of a handicapped child, she had known great trouble in her life, and had been able to share the problems not only with her first husband, who was the girl's father, but also with her second. Sadly, however, such tragedies may divide the partners rather than uniting them. One of the reasons for this may be that the circumstances prevent them from giving enough time to each other and from fully communicating how they feel about what is happening.

Joan Carter, writing in *We Believe in Marriage*, admits that she and her husband only really discovered what it meant to love and cherish when their baby was seriously ill, and she describes how they learnt to lean together on each other and Jesus. However, she acknowledged that when they started caring for their severely handicapped child at home, there was great danger of neglecting each other because the calls on their time were so great.

Many couples worry about how they would cope if a handicapped baby were born to them, and this is understandable, because even Christian marriages have been known to break under the strain.

Some people, on the other hand, feel able to offer to adopt or foster a handicapped child, and it goes without saying that both partners would need to feel equally committed to such action. Sara and Mike were a childless couple who adopted a girl of seven, having specified that if necessary they would accept a child with a minor physical problem. After a few years it emerged that their daughter's condition was more serious than anyone realised, and she had to have several operations to enable her to walk properly. Sara and Mike found that they could cope with these difficulties because the situation had arisen gradually, after they had grown used to being parents, just as it might have done with a child of their own.

Death of a child

If the greatest danger to a marriage with a handicapped child is lack of time for each other, the greatest danger if a child actually dies can be the danger of growing apart. In both cases, an irrational desire to blame yourself or your partner can arise – whose fault was it that the child was born like that? Whose fault that he had that accident or fell prey to that illness? This stems from a basic human need either to assume guilt or to apportion blame, and if it is deep-rooted it may need to be dealt with by a Christian counsellor. It can certainly be a death sentence to a marriage.

The death from leukaemia of their second daughter was a tragedy that Eileen Mitson and her husband shared, and in *We Believe in Marriage* she writes about its effect on their relationship. She talks of the regenerative quality of married love, in which touch can speak more than words, and of the powerful therapy of sexual union. Eileen and her husband were each deeply concerned about how the other would cope with this terrible loss, and they were able to express their love for each other in moments of deep misery. When a couple's marriage relationship is not so secure and they lose their only child, who may have acted as the main link between them, it is less likely that they will come through the experience with their marriage intact.

Sharon and James were not as spiritually close as the Mitsons because James did not totally share Sharon's Christian commitment, and she had often found that she had to cope with problems on her own. When they lost their second child at the age of a few months, they found that the tragedy brought them closer, and they were even able to pray together, which they didn't normally do. Sharon acknowledges that although the experience brought them closer together, it could have caused a rift in the marriage. She feels that the crucial factor was that they already had a child, and for her sake they had to keep going and not allow their mourning to lead them into wallowing in their grief. Sadly for Sharon, lovemaking served only to remind her of the baby they had so recently created – unlike Eileen Mitson who had lost a much older child.

Depression

In times of depression sexual love is most unlikely to be the bond which keeps the marriage together. A lack of interest in sex is one of the marks of depression, and this must therefore increase the chances of its having an adverse effect on the marriage. If you enjoy regular sex with your partner, you will find it difficult to adapt if this is withdrawn for some reason such as illness, absence, or very advanced pregnancy. If it is withheld simply because your husband, for example, 'doesn't feel like it', you may experience not only physical frustration but also rejection. It will be hard to understand that your husband is not actually going off you, but is unable to enjoy sex because he is ill with depression. In your attempt to help him, and to show that you still love him, you will want to draw close to him physically: if you are hurt when your advances are rejected you will, of course, only make your depressed husband feel more guilty and inadequate.

The trouble with depression is that those who don't suffer from it may find it hard to accept that it is as much a debilitating illness as asthma or a bad back. One might imagine that Christians should be better informed and more sympathetic, but sadly there are many circumstances in which a severely depressed Christian is allowed to feel guilty about his or her suffering – for is not the fruit of the Spirit love, *joy*, and peace? This can affect a marriage in two ways: if both husband and wife are Christians, the depressed one may be afraid of receiving this condemnatory attitude from the partner. If the sufferer is a Christian and the other is not, the Christian may be afraid of admitting how he or she feels, for fear of seeming a bad advertisement for the faith.

Even if communication in the marriage is good there will still be many problems. We have already touched on the fact that the sexual side of marriage is likely to suffer considerably. There may also be the problem, where a young woman is depressed, that the couple want to start trying for a baby but cannot, either because she is on anti-depressant drugs or because she is afraid of getting severe postnatal depression. Her condition may then become worse because she feels guilty about disappointing her husband in this area too.

Another result of depression is that sufferers usually wish to avoid company, and this means that they and probably their partner are likely to become cut off from their friends and perhaps even from fellowship at church. They are certainly unlikely to receive the attention that people with purely physical complaints do, when members of the church will often rally round and help with cooking, cleaning, child-minding, shopping, etc. This is partly because they make it clear that they don't want company, and partly because people are embarrassed by a psychosomatic illness and don't know what to say or do, or simply don't understand the extent of the disability. Either way, the sufferer may feel that nobody cares, and the partner will feel isolated.

It's beyond doubt that the husband or wife of a depressed person does have something considerable to cope with, and if you are in this situation you would benefit from reading Christian books on the subject, particularly *Coping with Depression* by Myra Chave-Jones. You should seek as much help, both medically and spiritually, as possible, and you should encourage your partner to believe that help is available and that they don't have to suffer alone. When your partner is very prone to depression you are not likely to escape without being affected yourself. When you do start to feel low you may then believe that you must hide it from your sick partner in order to spare him further anguish, and this of course can cause intolerable pressure.

Unemployment

A great deal of depression nowadays is caused by unemployment, because when it recurs or appears endless it is easy to lose hope. It is particularly difficult for a married man to be unemployed because he may feel that he is letting his wife and family down by failing to provide for them, and if the wife is not out at work they may get on top of each other in the home. As with other problems, it will either draw the partners closer together as they unite against their difficulties or create such intolerable pressures that they are driven apart. The same can happen when a self-employed person doesn't have enough work coming in, and the consequent worry and tension rubs off on his family.

When Len and Sonia got married it was the second time for both of them, and they were determined to make it work. Unfortunately Len was soon made redundant, and he felt very bad that Sonia had given up her job and her home to marry him and was now expecting his child, and he couldn't support her. Because of Sonia's very positive attitude, the struggle to make ends meet and the disappointments of job-hunting brought them closer together. Len appreciated this and was willing to be as much help to Sonia as he could. He shared the household jobs and the care of the children, and as he knew that this was a great advantage to her, he stopped feeling so useless.

It is strange how a couple may be drawn together by one problem but thrust apart by another. Tony and Marilyn found that coping with a child who didn't sleep made them so exhausted that their marriage suffered. They were going through a bad time because of this and had just had their worst ever quarrel, when Tony heard that he had been made redundant. This shock forced them to turn to the Lord and they resumed the neglected habit of praying together.

Because they both agreed that the problem was too big for them and they must go to God for help, they were able to rebuild their spiritual life both together and separately. Although Tony was never actually out of work, he did have to take a job away from home for a while, but by then they had become close enough to survive it and appreciated each other all the more at weekends. They both found that the separation enabled them to develop their personal spiritual lives more fully, with the result that their relationship with each other deepened.

Lindsay and Rod had a turbulent relationship and were planning to split up, when suddenly Lindsay was taken very ill. This served to repair the rift, since Rod had to start taking care of the children and running the home. Later, however, Rod suffered several periods of unemployment, and for them this was the major hurdle in the marriage. Whereas Len reacted to losing his job by worrying that he was letting his wife down, Rod responded by taking out his anger and frustration on Lindsay.

Childlessness

Earlier in this chapter we touched on the tragic subject of children dying; to those who have suffered this experience it might seem that the inability to have children is a much smaller problem. Those who are childless, however, may feel that 'it is better to have loved and lost than never to have loved'. Indeed, some people see childlessness as a kind of bereavement; one woman described how she had been particularly geared up to conceiving one month, and when her period came she sat and cried with the despair she would have felt if someone close to her had died. It is pointless to compare different kinds of sorrow and disappointment, and the fact remains that from the point of view of the marriage relationship, infertility is a grief which must be faced together. It is another situation in which sexual love may not be much comfort because many people find that the prolonged tests they have to undergo if they find they can't conceive make their sex life tense and artificial.

It is far more difficult to accept a problem and pray about it together if you don't both share the same attitude to it. The inability to identify with the way the other feels can cause communication problems that make the situation much worse. When Nichola married Clive she was eager to conceive. During six years of disappointment she became increasingly desperate to have a child and was beginning to get depressed. Clive felt no particularly strong paternal urge, so he had to learn to support Nichola in her depression and show that he was disappointed for her even though she knew he didn't mind so much for himself. After their first child was born Clive adapted easily to the role of father, so he was just as eager as his wife to have a second child. Consequently, when they again had to wait many years things were easier between them.

Clive and Nichola were among the lucky ones whose sorrow turned to joy when they found that subfertility was only temporary and not a final sentence. Writing in *Christian Woman* magazine, Ben Walsh described very sensitively not only the horror of the dawning realisation that a child may never materialise, but also the early stages of trying for a baby when he failed to appreciate the hurt his wife was feeling. She was shocked to find that she did not conceive as soon as they started trying, whereas he felt no sense of urgency and tried to reassure her that it would probably happen the following month.

Unfortunately men and women are unlikely to recognise their inherently differing attitudes to parenthood until either they have achieved that state or they have become reconciled to each other and to their infertility, by which time it is too late. Ben's wife continued to become tense and depressed until he offered 'spontaneous sorrow rather than unsympathetic rationality'. She was tempted to hate him for his lack of understanding, while he was frustrated because she was taking it so badly. They found it hard to talk and impossible to pray together. Fortunately they were able to see what was happening as the devil's attempt to destroy their marriage, and this enabled them to turn to each other and to the Lord. They realised that, although they had two views of the problem, God had only one and he would show them his will. By the time the final 'sentence' of childlessness came, they were close to each other mentally and spiritually.

Writing in the same article, Jane Young spoke of how involuntary childlessness is a kind of bereavement and how it puts a tremendous strain on a marriage:

> Guilt, resentment, shame at not being a 'real' man or woman, mixed with grief which can be very deep, conspire to tear a marriage apart. It takes patience, self-knowledge, forgiveness and self-forgiveness for a couple to go through the turmoil childlessness can bring and emerge still loving and trusting each other

Describing not so much the anxious years of trying to conceive, but the long years after the situation had been accepted, she mentions that many childless women live with a sense of futility which lies just under the surface and can engulf them at any minute. This means that the husband, who may have found it easier to get over his disappointment or who may never have felt it so keenly, will have to summon up a reserve of love and understanding whenever his wife enters one of the bad times.

Terminal illness
These differences in behaviour stem from our varying emotional needs. Other problems may arise because we are all at different stages in our spiritual development. Some people find it far easier to accept God's will than others, and although the initial reaction to bereavement, unemployment, infertility and other grief may nearly always be, 'Why, Lord?', some people continue to question God, whereas others come to realise that 'God's will hath no why', as Maria von Trapp was taught in her early days in the convent.

It is so difficult in marriage if one of you can accept the tragedy and the other can't, because then you may be unable to pray together just when you most need to. Communication will also be impaired if discussion of the subject leads to arguments, with one partner railing at God and the other 'defending' him.

This state of affairs created a very painful situation in our own home, since I am the kind of person who reacts with anger against God or whoever is available, while my husband accepts things more philosophically. A few months after the death of her husband, my mother-in-law, who had been a faithful Christian all her life, became very ill; although the doctors would not take her condition seriously to begin with, terminal cancer of the spine was eventually diagnosed. Before she died we had to come to terms with the fact that we were going to lose her, that she had been very badly treated by her doctors, and that her last months would be spent bedridden and in great pain. We were in a bad emotional state to receive this shock, since I had recently had a baby and soon became pregnant again, and John had never really had a chance to mourn for his father.

I think the worst thing was that it was such a long drawn-out death, that she was in such pain, and that by the end she had lost her sight. It was hard for both of us to believe that God could want a child of his to die in this way, and it made me wonder what kind of a Father he was. John, however, although he had great difficulty coming to terms with it, was eventually able to accept it as God's will, partly because his mother's continuing trust in the Lord was such an encouragement to others, and he emerged with his faith intact. If it had been my mother who was dying I would have felt justified in being the one who was shattered by it and who turned to my partner for support and comfort. But because it was John's mother, I felt that I should be the one to comfort and encourage and help him to cling on to his faith in God even in the darkest hour.

Because we did not have the same reaction to this tragedy, a spiritual rift grew between us. If I had been able to accept

78

the Lord's will in the way John did I could have been a support to him rather than a burden, and the suffering might have drawn us closer together instead of dividing us. It can be so easy to allow one tragedy to lead into a second one – a broken marriage.

Questions to ask

If a tragedy has caused your marriage relationship to deteriorate, is it because you are unconsciously blaming your partner?

Can you allow yourself and your partner to show grief and to share how you really feel about what is happening to you?

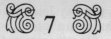 **7**

The Eternal Triangle

Many people become Christians in their teens and enjoy the heady atmosphere of a school or college Christian Union or a thriving youth group at their church, and they have the chance to attend Christian camps and house-parties. They become used to praying with their friends, and when they start to date someone seriously it is likely that that boy or girl is already a member of their group. It is very easy to form a spiritual relationship at that age, and praying with your fiancé is a natural progression from praying with him in the company of others. John and I found that our Christian friends at university who got engaged before they left were more likely to remain committed and active in their faith than those who went out into the world without a Christian partner beside them.

It may be ideal to meet your soul-mate in these circumstances and establish your marriage in this way. But unfortunately it is also true that the higher you start, the further you have to fall. It can be an awful shock to find yourselves as a newly married couple, perhaps in new jobs, a new home and a new church – now too old for the youth club and far away from the fellowship of the Christian Union. With the responsibilities of running a house and holding down a job, or coping with unemployment, and later on perhaps with the arrival of babies, the spiritual atmosphere is very different, and far more determination is needed than you would have expected, to keep alive your relationship with God.

If you have become a Christian after your marriage, the

greatest problem must be if your partner is not converted. Even when you both come to the Lord at the same time, however, life is not likely to be easy, because so many adjustments will have to be made. You each have to establish your own relationship with God at the same time as readjusting to a spiritual relationship with each other and explaining the change to your friends and relations. You might benefit from having a sort of sabbatical year together, or a prolonged second honeymoon, in which you curtail your activities (rather than taking on new ones at church) sufficiently to allow time to get used to the changes in each other and the idea of living as Christians.

It is very easy to say that marriage is an 'eternal triangle' with husband and wife at the base, both linking up to Jesus at the apex, but it is so difficult in practice to treat the Lord as if he were the third person in the marriage. Sometimes it may seem as if you and your husband are having a tug-of-war with both hands on the base line, having quite let go of your link with the apex. At other times the spiritual side of marriage may cause problems and jealousies, almost as if it were the other kind of infamous eternal triangle. In other words, whether you are a newly converted couple in your fifties or a young pair who met at the college CU, your spiritual life together is not likely to be a bed of roses.

Friends or enemies?

The period following my mother-in-law's death was a very difficult one for us, bringing changes in many aspects of our life – a change of job, adapting to a new baby, and different responsibilities at church. Our joint spiritual life had reached such a low ebb that every time anything came up to do with the church or Christianity in general it would cause an argument, whether it was a policy decision at a church meeting, the interpretation of a passage of Scripture, accepting guidance, or taking on another job at church. The latter caused the greatest problems. It seemed to me that my husband was taking on more and more, either to prove what a good Christian he was or to annoy me, whereas it seemed to him that I deliberately opposed everything he tried to do in the church, as well as challenging everything he believed. It really felt as if an intruder was trying to break up our marriage.

One night, when the situation had become particularly acute, I received enlightenment on what I believed to be – and what John at length admitted *could* be – the root cause of the whole problem. When his mother's illness was diagnosed I reacted very badly, as I have already said, and could not accept the concept of a loving Father making one of his children suffer in this way. Normally my husband would have helped me through this problem and we would have drawn strength for my wavering faith from his firmer beliefs. In these circumstances, however, he was himself so shattered that he only just managed to survive with his own faith intact, and it was very important for him to preserve his trust in God in order to encourage his mother to keep hold of hers.

Whenever I gave voice to my unhelpful feelings I was tempting him to relapse into antipathy towards God. This would have been no help to him or his mother, so he had to 'arm' himself against my attitude and resist it so that he did not lose spiritual ground. Unfortunately he became so accustomed, during those difficult months, to looking upon me as a spiritual antagonist that the habit persisted. I became used to him arguing with everything I said about Christianity and came to think of our faith as something which divided rather than united us. For that reason I began to resent any 'religious' activity he became involved in, whether a job in the church or even a prolonged time of Bible study, while he became very defensive and reacted without trying to empathise when I challenged anything he was doing, which of course created an even worse reaction in me.

Recognising that we were caught in this dreadful vicious circle certainly didn't solve the problem, but it made it much easier for me to accept it. I knew that I had not been helpful during the period of sickness and bereavement, and it seemed quite reasonable that our complex problems should have stemmed from the tensions during that time. When I realised that my husband was subconsciously treating me as a spiritual antagonist I asked him to stop. At first he wouldn't admit it, but at least it was brought to the front of his mind so that he was more likely to be aware of it.

I should like to be able to say that we then sat down together to pray about the mess we were in, but things don't work like that when the whole point is that you have passed the stage at which you can pray together. However, we both prayed about it separately, and gradually things began to improve. Not many people are likely to have a problem the same as ours, but it illustrates the basic point that no problem can be solved until it is defined.

Guidance
Someone remarked to me recently that it must be lovely to have a Christian marriage. I wished I could have said, 'Yes, it's fantastic', but I had to admit that as well as experiencing great joy, Christians have pressures in their marriages which non-Christians don't have and these make it harder to achieve the perfect triangle that a Christian marriage should be. One pressure has already been dealt with – that of fitting church commitments into an already full schedule of priorities; another problem can be not having enough in common except your faith, and that will be covered in chapter 9.

A further aspect of life which can create tension for Christian couples is accepting guidance. It might seem that the Christians are at a considerable advantage here, because they can turn to God to guide them, but it is only an advantage if you and your partner can be united about seeking God's guidance and recognising it when it comes. The fortunate Christian couple who have a good spiritual relationship will automatically pray together at every turning point in their life and should be able to agree on accepting the signs that God gives. If, however, you find it difficult to pray together, you may also find it difficult to accept any guidance that one of you may feel you have received.

When John and I have been through bad spiritual patches, it has always annoyed me when he has said to people, 'We prayed about this course of action and felt God leading us into it.' In fact *we* had not prayed at all as a couple, and he had just assumed that I had been praying about the same subject, and that I had received the same answer. When he decided to give up his job without having anything else lined up to go to, I found it almost impossible to believe that God wanted him to take such an irresponsible step. Yet because he insisted that this was God's plan, I felt that I was going against the Lord every time I questioned the wisdom of the move. A friend married to a non-Christian agreed with me that in these circumstances her lot would be easier because someone without a faith would not be likely to take such a risky step, and certainly wouldn't be able to justify it.

I don't know whether my husband was guided by God in what he did, but I do know that if we had been in the habit of praying together it is likely that I would have been able to accept it better. I learned, however, from Ann England, writing in *We Believe in Marriage*, that a wife will not necessarily receive direct guidance and must trust God in her husband. This does not mean that the husband should 'go it alone' and exclude his wife from prayers and decisions. When Edward England felt the Lord telling him to resign from his position in the publishing world, without another job in view, Ann didn't know whether God was in it or not, but he prayed about it with her and wanted her to be sure too. Because of his consideration and their close spiritual relationship, she was able to trust God in him and set him free to follow the path he felt he should take.

Praying together
The very fact that a great deal of advice is given about praying as a couple, and also with the children, can put an extra strain on a marriage. Not only are we expected to live amicably together, to go out to work, to run the home, to

be faithful, and so on, but we are also expected to pray together, and if we don't, then we are made to feel that our marriage is lacking something. The more we hear that 'the family that prays together stays together' the more we worry about what will befall our family if we don't, and the more guilty we feel about admitting to this gap in our family activities. Often we hear and read so much about devotional times in the home that we assume that every family except ours excels in this area, and it can be very helpful to get together with a few other couples to share any problems. When John and I did this we were surprised at how many others found this side of the family life difficult. It was interesting to know that many felt that the important thing was to encourage children to pray and read the Bible for themselves rather than insisting on rather artificial family devotions, especially if the children are far apart in age.

Regarding praying together as a Christian couple, our marriage *is* lacking something if we don't do it, but then so it is if we don't enjoy sex as much as we might, or if we have no hobbies or interests in common. It is the quality of our individual private times of prayer that determines the quality of our Christian life, and if we find it hard to pray with our partner (or children) we should not be singled out for particular criticism any more than if we had given up having intercourse. Sadly, some Christians who are brave enough to admit to having a less-than-perfect marriage are simply met with the answer that everything would be fine if they started praying together, as if that were something that could be accomplished as easily as going for a walk together. On the other hand, the inability to pray together should not be brushed aside, particularly as it may be the symptom, rather than the cause, of some deep problem.

For many years Wendy had not been able to pray aloud with her husband, Nick. This had come quite easily when they were students but as the marriage wore on – perhaps after they had let praying together lapse for a while – she discovered that she couldn't do it. To Wendy – as to me – praying with your husband is mid-way between praying

85

alone and praying in a group of people. Because you are not alone, you don't pour your heart out incoherently to God as you might in your private prayer times, but you feel the situation is too intimate to formulate a prayer in the way you might do in a meeting.

Unfortunately, Nick regarded her reluctance – nay, refusal – to pray out loud as unwillingness to have a prayer time together, and he said he didn't see why he should always be the one to put the prayers into words. Wendy felt guilty about her shortcomings and was always fearful of a prayer time being suggested because she knew Nick would put pressure on her to pray. Eventually they also were helped by talking the problem over in a group, and they were surprised to find that it was quite common for the husband to be the only one who prayed out loud, even among couples who were both very spiritually mature. This made Nick realise that Wendy's request was not so odd after all, and she began to feel less guilty, so they both approached the idea of praying together feeling more relaxed. Though they claim they are still not good at it, they have certainly succeeded more than before. They discuss what they want to pray about, Nick prays out loud, and Wendy says 'amen', and now that she no longer feels under pressure, she has very occasionally had the courage to add a few words of her own.

Left behind

Susan and Tom had both been divorced, and became Christians around the time they married each other. They found that their faith was a great help in their life together. They both felt quite natural about it and were able to pray together spontaneously and share their faith with others in the normal course of conversation. They became closer in every way than they had been to their previous partners, and with the help of the James Dobson *Focus on the Family* films Susan was able to analyse herself and get rid of some of the hang-ups which impeded earlier relationships.

The advantage that Susan and Tom had was that they

became Christians together and were therefore at the same stage and able to grow together. Many couples have problems because one of them gets left behind spiritually – either because they don't share their partner's faith at all, or because one has entered into a deeper spiritual experience which the other feels unable to share. If a Christian has married a non-Christian they should have envisaged these problems from the start, but many get married without receiving any teaching or advice on the subject. In any case, even if they were wrong in their choice of partner, they still need to be encouraged to make a go of the marriage.

Where one partner becomes a Christian after they are married there can be even more problems, because the non-Christian would be justified in claiming that the person he or she had married has changed. It seems to be most often the wife who becomes a Christian first (or a girl who chooses a non-Christian partner); if it were the other way round it would be easier, and more consistent with his role as head of the house, for the husband to try gently to lead his wife to the Lord. When he is not a Christian it is very difficult for her to regard him as the leader in the marriage when he cannot lead in spiritual matters, and overenthusiastic efforts by the wife to convert her husband may make it appear that she is trying to dominate him. It is important in these cases that the church's involvement should be as far as possible with the *couple*, for it is very easy for a woman who goes to church on her own to be treated by the congregation as if she were single. It is also essential that the husband should not be able to accuse the fellowship (or worse still any of the male spiritual leaders in it) of trying to take his wife away from him. A number of books have been written to help women whose husbands do not share their faith, for example *Loving God, Loving You* by Marion Stroud, or *The Tug of Two Loves* by Meg Scott.

Although women seem to find it easier than men to make a decision for the Lord, when both are already Christians it is often the man who progresses faster than his wife to deeper spiritual experiences. This may particularly be the case if he is involved in leadership in the fellowship or if he goes alone to a number of meetings because she is at home coping with young children. The baptism in the Holy Spirit, though essentially a beautifully unifying experience for Christians of different denominations, can also be divisive if those who have not received it are suspicious of the gifts or if those who have had the experience become a spiritual clique. This can happen in a church and also within a marriage, and I would suggest that, if one partner is living on a much higher spiritual plane than the other, there may be as many problems as if one is a Christian and the other not. For years I was afraid for us as a couple to pray for the baptism in the Holy Spirit because I felt sure that John would receive it before I did and that he would change so much that I would lose him: such fears may seem foolish to some people, but they are real to those who experience them and should not be brushed aside.

Any couple who have this sort of problem should read Caroline Urquhart's book *His God, My God*, in which she describes with great honesty and humility her feelings of fear and resentment when her husband became deeply involved in the work of the Holy Spirit in his parish. Caroline was struggling to live as a Christian in her own strength, while Colin had been filled with the Spirit and was leading many people in the fellowship into this experience and also exercising many of the gifts of the Spirit, including healing and speaking in tongues. His wife seemed to have got left behind on the first rung of the ladder (which could have been due to his insensitivity or her obstinacy) and the more she saw people overtake her and start worshipping with Colin in the Spirit, the less she wanted to catch up.

Eventually, it was another clergyman, a friend of Colin's, who was able to counsel Caroline and lead her to a real experience of all three persons of the Trinity. Colin commented that he obviously wasn't much use as her vicar and would concentrate on being her husband, and she replied that she preferred him that way. This is very significant because it shows that although Caroline has a good marriage relationship with Colin – or perhaps because of it – at that particular time she needed someone else to be her spiritual teacher. (This is just as understandable as some women not having their husbands to teach them to drive!)

The other side of the coin
One of the difficulties about having a spiritual relationship with your husband or wife is that you know each other so well and see every side of each other. Some people seem to be very uncomplicated, and show the same sort of personality whether they are at church, at work, playing golf or making a cake. These I privately categorise as 'one person'. 'Two people', on the other hand, are those who, although their complexity may make them more interesting, are actually inconsistent because they have a 'Sunday face' (as one friend describes it) which they put on for church services, Bible studies, prayer groups and so on, and an ordinary side which is seen the rest of the time. They may also have a third side for work.

It is not that these people mean to be hypocritical, or that they swear and get drunk when they are not in Christian circles, or do anything inconsistent with their faith. It is just that, often without realising it, they reserve a certain manner of speech – inflection and vocabulary – and a certain facial expression, for when they are involved in spiritual activities. I always know when John is going to bring up a spiritual topic of conversation because his voice changes as soon as he starts to speak, and when he is leading a service or Bible study he puts on his special Sunday smile! On such occasions I sit there cringing, not because of what he is saying or doing, but because the person saying it is just not *him*.

I am sure that many wives of clergymen, lay preachers and other church leaders must have difficulty listening to their husbands' sermons, and this is a pity because these women give out so much that they may be even more in need of encouragement and spiritual refreshment than everyone else. Some feel that a wife should if possible go to a different house group from the one her husband leads (or even attends). This would have to depend on the couple, but I feel it should be a last resort as it would encourage them to form spiritual relationships with different people, which could be divisive if problems needed to be shared. Helen's husband David does a lot of lay preaching, and although he is undeniably 'one person' she still has problems. For example, when he used to lead a Bible study she would get very upset when awkward members of the group tried to disrupt the discussion. At one time she used to find herself always criticising his preaching, but after a while she was able to get something out of it; however, she still cannot help worrying about any minor aspects of the service which go wrong when he is preaching.

Caroline Urquhart writes that she had difficulty accepting that the person with whom she had a close physical relationship was also a great spiritual leader. She found it impossible to accept that Colin's hands, which had been used by God for laying on people for healing and deliverance, could also be used to embrace and caress her. Another vicar remarked that his wife had difficulty seeing him as 'one person', and her problem was in accepting that the man in the pulpit was the same as the one who made love to her.

The spiritual and physical relationships between married people are obviously very closely interlinked, and both need to be carefully analysed if problems are to be solved. So we shall go on to look at the way our spiritual state as Christians is likely to affect our sexuality.

Questions to ask

Is there any unresolved conflict between you which is poisoning your spiritual togetherness?

How would you know if your partner was feeling left behind spiritually and therefore felt excluded?

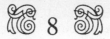

8

No Sex, Please, We're Christians!

Why should people think that sexuality is inconsistent with spirituality? Why should sex be made out to be a dirty word rather than one of God's greatest creations? Why should the injunction to 'Thank God for sex' cause a couple any problems? The sexual act was invented by God, and all married Christians should be able to thank him for it and to appreciate the wonder of being united with another person both physically and spiritually. However, the abuse of sex in the secular world by pornography, vulgar language and jokes, and particularly by perverted practices and sexual crimes, has given it so many unpleasant connotations that it can be difficult for a Christian to see it as a pure gift of God.

Indentifying the problems
Whatever the causes of problems in the area of sex and the spiritual life, and however unreasonable they may sound, the fact is that they do exist for some people, and to ignore them or refuse to discuss them can only make matters worse. Alison and Peter who had been married for several years and had two children, had reached a point at which neither their sex life nor their spiritual relationship was as good as it might have been. Alison explained to Peter that she was becoming aware that she couldn't feel right having a spiritual and a sexual relationship with the same person. They talked about it from time to time but could see no solution; Alison also shared it with a close Christian friend who was sympathetic and encouraging but had no easy answer.

In the years that followed, their spiritual relationship became worse. Peter would complain at intervals that it was very bad that they didn't pray together, but he never made a serious effort to do anything about it. Alison felt that as he was the spiritual head of the house he should instigate regular prayer times, and because he only talked about it but didn't do anything she felt he was being hypocritical. Sexually their relationship had its high and low points, but after a while it began to improve considerably. Because their spiritual togetherness had dwindled to virtually nothing, Alison was able to put the conflict to the back of her mind and to be glad that their marriage was improving in one respect at least.

One evening they were discussing marriage problems in general with a few friends, and Peter mentioned Alison's hang-up and the restrictions it had placed on their relationship. Suddenly they realised that this had been the reason for Peter's reluctance to insist on having prayer together. At the back of his mind he knew that for Alison it was either prayer *or* sex, so every night that he suggested praying together (they were people who didn't function well in the mornings) he was doing himself out of any sexual activity. Alison realised that her husband had strong sexual needs and that he was pleased that their sex life was improving, so it was easy for her to understand that he had been unwilling to jeopardise this by suggesting regular prayer times. She was therefore able to stop accusing him of being hypocritical, and this gave her more desire to improve their spiritual relationship. Because they had managed to recognise their subconscious attitude to the problem, they were able to rectify it.

Some people assumed that Alison's conflict had been due to a Puritanical upbringing in which sex was regarded as a necessary evil, but this was not the case – in fact, if anything, it was Peter who had been taught to think in that way. Before they were married, Alison and Peter had an easy spiritual relationship and such a good physical one that they found difficulty in restraining themselves from having intercourse. When they married they did have some problems, possibly due to the unnatural restraints they had been under, and maybe their later conflict was due to the fact that sex had not turned out to be the natural, easy relationship they had expected.

Origins of the problems
Young Christians who don't have problems about their pre-marital sexual activities are fortunate. There are three traps they could fall into: they could be tempted to be more intimate than they should, or they might try to subdue the physical side of the relationship altogether. Thirdly, there is the situation just described, in which two healthy and passionate young people create a great build-up as the sexual act is eagerly awaited. However close they become physically, they always manage to stop short of intercourse, but in their frustration at never reaching a satisfactory climax, their petting becomes more and more intense and frequent. By the time they marry they have built intercourse up to be so desirable that they are bound to be disappointed by it, or the tension they are feeling may prevent them from achieving full intercourse at all. When the forbidden fruit suddenly becomes available it may automatically lose some of its glamour, and the couple who used to indulge in heavy petting every evening may find they only make love once a week. This will feel unnatural to them and they will wonder what has gone wrong.

Some would say that the answer to this problem is more self-control before marriage and a shorter engagement, but circumstances often make the latter impossible. As for self-control, if the couple find that too easy it may be that they are not sufficiently attracted physically and shouldn't be getting married. They can, of course, pray that God will help them to keep their passions in check, but then they will have to be sure to change their prayers quickly upon marriage and start asking God to allow them to enjoy each other without inhibition.

Looking back, Alison and Peter realised that they had

been more intimate in some ways during their engagement than some people are after marriage, and that it had been rather artificial to draw the line at intercourse. The only difference that would have made was the danger of pregnancy which was highly unlikely anyway, with responsible contraception. Because of this, some engaged Christian couples do decide to have sex before marriage, maintaining that this is not adultery (where one partner is already married) or fornication (which they claim means sleeping around rather than with someone you love). There are, of course, many arguments against this. Most Christians would point out that the Bible does mean that any pre-marital sex is wrong; that even the most reliable contraceptive can fail; that the engagement might break up, and so on. Another problem is that, if the ultimate sexual union is achieved before marriage, it may cloud the young people's judgement of other aspects of their relationship and they may feel less free to admit that they are not really suited and to break off an unwise engagement.

Advice on where to draw the line in physical courtship and a much more profound treatment of pre-marital relations will be found in books specifically dealing with the subject, such as *Growing into Love* by Joyce Huggett, which should be helpful to younger people. For our purposes, we consider it only to assess the effect of guilt on the married couple's future sexual relationship. If you were not Christians during the engagement, you will presumably feel that any sexual excesses were forgiven with your other sins when you came to the Lord, but it is not that easy if you were already believers and now realise that you deliberately went against what God would want. It is important to remember that Jesus' blood was shed for the sins we commit after we come to him as well as before, and that confession and repentance can free us from memories of the past.

You may well be horrified at any suggestion that Christians could consider sex before marriage or even indulge in heavy petting. In that case you will obviously avoid the problems mentioned so far, but may find you enter marriage without being sufficiently certain of your physical desire for each other and without having talked about your feelings on sex and contraception. (This, of course, can happen to non-Christians as well, but it is more often in Christian homes, where there is – rightly – a horror of modern permissiveness, that young people are brought up to see any kind of sexual contact before marriage as wrong.) It is not surprising, then, if it takes them a while to relax and accept sex as a gift from God. They should also read widely on the subject – before marriage is obviously best, but it is never too late to start!

Selwyn Hughes, in *Marriage as God Intended*, describes the way in which sex used to be downgraded by the Church in the middle ages and was regarded by some people as a sin even within marriage. He mentions the continuing belief that a few Christians have, even nowadays, that it is something God frowns upon. Anne Townsend, in *Marriage without Pretending*, also quotes examples of people who have this problem. Even some Christians who do not share these fallacious views and who have a healthy relationship with each other seem to regard sex as the 'poor relation' in their marriage. Of course, it is good if a marriage is so strong in other respects that it can survive whether sex is a major factor or not, but it seems sad if people are not gaining the full enjoyment from this side of marriage, just as it is if they cannot share deeply on a spiritual or emotional level.

Sex in the media
When a Christian couple can be relaxed about sex and thank God for it and even pray that he will give them a fuller enjoyment of each other, then they should be able to participate without inhibition in any form of lovemaking acceptable to both of them. The trouble is that the all-pervasive media distort sex, and twisted images can crowd into the mind so that the purity of married love can easily be spoilt. The so-called 'soft porn' magazines with provocative pictures of halfclad women on the cover can make a woman feel reticent about arousing her husband by wearing sexy

95

attire. It is also difficult to enjoy sex if your mind is full of reports of rape, prostitution, child abuse, homosexuality, and other perversions which are frequently featured on the news.

It is not feasible – nor would it be right – to cut ourselves off from all contact with the world, but we can cut the world out of our bedroom by asking God to take these unpleasant thoughts from our minds. He will do this because he wants us to have the freedom to enjoy his gift to us. It's usually the wife whose mind is distracted by more than one train of thought, and you may need to pray that you will not be disturbed by any outside influence or train of thought, however wholesome.

Whereas Christians will inevitably hear about the abuse of sex in news items, we should obviously never choose to watch any film or play of a pornographic nature because this is a total misuse of God's gift. Some books and television programmes of course, while not being pornographic, do have a significant sexual content, and what one Christian finds acceptable another Christian will not feel free to watch. Each of us must set our own standards. If you find that you have been 'turned on' by what you have been watching or reading – and especially if you have both been experiencing it – then take advantage of the feeling and make love to each other without further ado! In this way, the content of the story will not have left you with impure thoughts but will have enabled you to express your love for each other (provided of course that you are thinking of your partner at the time, and not of the attractive person on the television).

Sexual fantasies can often make Christians feel guilty and frustrated, but when you are married you should be able to ask God to help you turn them to good account. Barbara was on holiday with her husband – this is a rare example of a relationship improving on holiday instead of deteriorating – and was feeling relaxed and having more time than usual for reading. She realised that the historical drama she was engrossed in was encouraging her to go to sleep weaving sexual fantasies which would then often be reflected in her dreams. Her first reaction was to feel guilty, but she then realised that God had given her the ability to give vent to her passionate feelings. When next her mind was filled in this way, she approached her husband (instead of waiting, as she usually did, for him to make the first move) and amazed and delighted him by her unexpected display of passion.

Making the most of it

Feelings of sexual desire, as well as being stimulated by what we read or see, can also be brought on by circumstances – an unexpected evening out together or turning to each other for comfort. Equally, the sudden feelings can be caused by our physical or mental state at any time – for example, pregnancy or a certain point in the menstrual cycle, or perhaps a special feeling of wellbeing. It is a good thing to take advantage of these feelings when they occur, even if it means stopping the car in a deserted lay-by one dark evening and making love on the back seat!

Such an extreme departure from normal married sex would naturally have to be totally acceptable to both of you, but it is good to try to accommodate your partner even if you prefer more conventional lovemaking. For example, many people think that intercourse can only take place in bed, at bedtime, with the light out, whereas some would like the freedom to let an embrace on the sofa turn into a lovemaking session (provided of course that no one can barge into the room!). As far as the time of day is concerned, it may be more logical to make love last thing at night and then drift into a deep sleep, but if the urge overtakes you during the day and if you have the opportunity, it is a pity to wait for the night when the feeling may have passed or you may be too tired. Men are more easily aroused by sight than women, so any wife who is able to overcome a basic reluctance to have the light on may be doing her husband a big favour.

Of course, there is no reason for all lovemaking to be done

to suit the one who favours unconventional circumstances – there must be give and take on both sides. The same applies to the way in which it is done; one of you may appreciate a long drawn out session and the other may prefer it to be brief and passionate. In time you should both be able to appreciate all aspects of lovemaking; if you have not chosen the circumstances yourself, you can at least gain satisfaction from the pleasure you are giving to your partner. It is also important to be able to make use of the different 'moods' for lovemaking – passionate, gentle, playful, serious and so on – and to be sensitive to your partner's needs in this respect.

Unfortunately, much sexual frustration can occur during pregnancy, and yet in some cases this time can present unexpected opportunities for enjoyment. Many people stop having intercourse in the early months, either because the wife feels unwell or because they are afraid (in a few cases justifiably) of causing a miscarriage. Obviously if you are advised at any stage of pregnancy to refrain from intercourse you should take that advice, and it may be easier to do this if you ask the doctor to explain exactly what the danger is.

Generally, however, during the middle and later months there is no medical reason for not enjoying sex, and there are books containing fascinating diagrams illustrating ways of allegedly achieving sexual union in spite of the bulge! Some women feel particularly sexy at this time: they have a feeling of general wellbeing and elation as well as a sense of achievement, and they don't need to worry about either contraception or the need to conceive. Many men feel proud to see their wife's shape heralding, as it does, the arrival of their child, and they find an added excitement in their physical relationship; but sadly, some are involuntarily turned off at the thought of making love to an obviously pregnant woman. Such a situation needs to be treated with considerable understanding, and if the man really cannot overcome his feelings he should not underestimate the hurt his wife might be experiencing as he appears to reject her.

Peace of mind

The months after a baby is born are almost bound to be difficult ones for your sex life. You will probably have abstained from intercourse for a few weeks before and after the birth, so your husband may be getting rather frustrated, while you will have had so many physical and emotional changes to cope with that sex may be far from your mind. As the months go by you may still find it difficult to relax and to be singleminded about lovemaking (the baby is almost bound to cry just as you are under way!) but for your husband's sake you should not refuse altogether. He, in turn, should be grateful for what sexual satisfaction you can give him and not expect you to be back to normal for some time. If you are quite uninterested he must realise that it is sex in general that you are against, and not him in particular.

Several couples whose babies were bad sleepers report that this put paid to their sex life for some time, because they were just too tense and exhausted to enjoy it. This is quite understandable, although it might be an idea to take advantage of any unexpected lull and try making love. As at other times of trial it could turn out to have more of a healing effect than otherwise. Some women find that their sexual desire decreases when they are breast-feeding, and couples who have their child sleeping in the same room may find this rather inhibiting.

Another thing which may spoil sexual enjoyment at this time is the fear of getting pregnant again, especially if you have not made a decision about long-term contraception since having the baby, and certainly nothing is more inhibiting to sexual enjoyment than the fear of an unwanted pregnancy. As the years go by it may be necessary to change your method of contraception; Gail Lawther in her book *Family Planning* gives a very helpful summary of all the available methods, with a list of questions to enable readers to see which might be the most appropriate for them at any particular time. Obviously it is important for complete agreement to be reached especially in the case of sterilisation, which is so final. It is easy for feelings of guilt and regret to arise and damage a relationship if one partner feels they have agreed to something against their will.

Even when you think you have come to a considered agreement, you may find you have been mistaken about your real feelings. Ruth and Eddie had talked for some years about being sterilised when they reached their mid-thirties, and after much discussion they had agreed that Eddie should have the operation rather than Ruth. When they reached that age, they had four children as planned and were using a contraceptive which they found acceptable and reliable. As the youngest child neared a year old it seemed sensible for Eddie to be sterilised. They had proved that they were very fertile and they definitely felt they shouldn't have more children and wouldn't be able to cope with them. They talked to a few Christian friends about it and certainly prayed, but more along the lines of, 'This is what we're doing; is that OK, God?' Eddie had the operation and experienced no doubts or regrets, but Ruth was immediately assailed by worry and guilt. She felt quite sure that they had been wrong and began to think that one of the children would die 'as a punishment'. She also found she had less faith in the vasectomy than in their previous contraceptives.

Eddie might have been forgiven for being very impatient with this reaction, since he had gone through the pain of the operation, but fortunately he was able to see that his wife was really upset and let her talk out her fears. He was even willing to go back to taking other precautions if that would restore her peace of mind. Finally they agreed to wait for many months more than the doctors required before Eddie had his final test; after that they would stop using contraceptives gradually. Ruth realised that she had been at fault in agreeing to the operation, because she was the one whose conscience was not (and in fact never had been) at peace about it, and it was not an issue on which Eddie wanted to exercise his headship and take the full responsibility.

Ruth came to believe that God had forgiven her and that

it was not in his nature to punish them by taking one of their children from them. Fortunately, because Eddie had been so sensitive, their sexual relationship was not adversely affected, but if he had dismissed Ruth's worries and fears as groundless she could have become a very unwilling lover.

Individuality
Sensitivity and the acceptance of the fact that your partner has very individual feelings and desires is surely the hallmark of a successful sexual relationship. This, I feel, should be borne in mind when reading books on sex, such as Tim La Haye's *The Act of Marriage*, which is a very detailed book written from both a Christian and a medical point of view. This book is extremely helpful for people who are entering marriage and for those who are married and want to improve their physical relationship, but it should be remembered that any book of this kind is bound to generalise and talk about what applies to the majority. God made us all as individuals, and not everyone will react in the same way to a certain form of physical touch, any more than they will all enjoy something that most people find beautiful.

For example, most writers on sex will agree that a man is aroused more quickly and often wants to have intercourse long before his wife is fully participating and certainly before she is ready to reach a climax. However, some women are different, and a man who spends a long time leading up to sex because he thinks he is pleasing his wife may find that she is getting impatient and frustrated. Similarly, a woman can't expect her husband to be instantly turned on just because the books say he will be. If he is the one who needs longer foreplay, then that is simply his individuality. The fact that a woman actually dislikes the very form of stimulation which the books advise the husband to use does not mean that she is frigid or weird – it simply means that they both need to find out what works for her.

As in everything else, the key is communication, and it is well worth working to achieve this, even if it is difficult at first. Remember that it is probably far easier to talk about intimate matters in bed in the dark than in any other situation.

In addition to discussing their feelings dispassionately, some people like to talk about their sexual union while it is happening, but others find such communication quite off-putting, even if they are not normally embarrassed about discussing sex. We know from the Song of Solomon that it is not wrong to put your feelings and desires into words and you may find it helpful to read this beautiful passage of Scripture before (or during or after) lovemaking. On the other hand, if someone finds the use of explicit sexual references distasteful they should tell their partner, so that they can work through the problem together instead of allowing it to alienate them.

Sex in the bad times
Another way in which individuality is shown in a marriage is the attitude to sex during the bad times: is a bad sexual relationship a *cause* of a worsening marriage or a *result* of it? Except in the cases where both partners place little value on the physical side of the relationship (genuinely, and not just saying it to please the other), there is little doubt that if all is not well in bed, that will probably be affecting other aspects of life as well. Therefore, if the sexual problems are not of a temporary nature (for example, concern about becoming pregnant) it is advisable to seek professional counselling.

But what about the converse? If the marriage is going through a bad patch for other reasons, need we expect the sexual side to suffer as a result? We have seen that in cases of loss and shared grief, tender sexual union can be a comfort because you are turning to each other in your distress. If, however, your problems are among the others mentioned in this book – disagreement over spiritual matters or in-laws, tension caused by money worries or too many calls on your time, for example, you may find yourselves turning away from, rather than towards, each other in your misery. Unfortunately, to allow this to happen will only create further tension in the form of frustrated sexual desires and could make both of you more susceptible to the temptation of an extra-marital relationship.

However, this need not happen, and it is possible to use sex as a sort of safety valve when the tension becomes too great. Derek and Vicky found that in many ways their marriage entered a bad patch after they became Christians. It may have been because of the pressure of being given too many jobs in the church, or because the devil wanted to destroy their union, or perhaps it hadn't ever been that good in the first place, but they hadn't realised it. Their sex life, however, improved because they felt a new freedom to talk about it, and this improvement continued despite a general (fortunately temporary) deterioration which nearly led to separation.

Paul and Lucy also went through a difficult year in their marriage, with money worries, spiritual problems and inordinate calls on their time, and they too considered separation, but they actually found that their sexual relationship improved. Lucy realised that when they had not made love for several days, Paul's already frayed temper became significantly worse, and she knew that after intercourse they would both be more relaxed for a while. Paul was also suffering from slight depression, and had many worries, and this made him less likely to instigate sexual contact, so Lucy (who had never taken the lead before) forced herself to initiate lovemaking. She told Paul that she needed him (which was true), and he was so pleasantly surprised at her advances that he soon responded, and they found that all the frustrations and tensions in the other aspects of life were released. Their lovemaking became increasingly passionate and satisfactory to both, so that when they assessed their marriage, as they frequently did, and wondered if it could survive, they had to admit that in one respect at least it was doing more than surviving – it was flourishing!

This was not, of course, the whole answer to Lucy and Paul's problems, and they couldn't have lived at that highly-charged pitch for ever, but if they had allowed the physical side of their marriage to deteriorate as well, they would have had even further to go to put their marriage back together again. Some people might criticise their attitude and say that they were using intercourse in a cold-blooded manner instead of allowing it to be sparked off by feelings of passionate love. Most people would say that sex is an excellent way of making up after a quarrel but that they wouldn't feel like doing it in the middle of a row (in spite of evidence to the contrary on many television dramas!), and I would go along with that. Lucy and Paul didn't ever have intercourse during their many violent slanging matches, but simply when they felt miserable, tense and alienated.

I see no scriptural reason for believing that this is wrong; indeed in 1 Corinthians 7:5 Paul says, 'Do not deprive each other . . .'. Sexual union has both physical and psychological connotations, and if one or both of you feel that you need it for psychological release, surely it would be wrong to deny it. We believe that love and marriage go together and that sex is wrong if you are in love but not married; should we believe it is also bad if you are married but no longer in love? Perhaps it is if you are finally separated and awaiting divorce; if you are still trying to make a go of marriage but feel you have no love left, you can ask God to give you love (see chapter 11). If you believe you can still have love for each other, there is no need to feel that any sexual activity is wrong.

Lucy and Paul were totally honest with each other about their reasons for instigating sex, and they came to realise that it was important to make love every time one of them wanted to. So even though in many respects they were not at one with each other, they did avoid any temptation to sexual infidelity.

Questions to ask

Are you and your partner really able to thank God for sex together?

Do you have any worries or disagreements about birth control which need to be resolved?

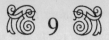

9

Unfaithful in More Ways than One

The seventh commandment is probably the most often quoted of the ten, and the word 'adultery', whether uttered in a disapproving manner or made the subject of a joke, is always given its full sexual connotation. However, 'adultery' actually means breaking the marriage vows, and since our vows obviously involve a great deal more than sex, I believe that breaking a marriage relationship on some other level can also be regarded as a kind of adultery.

A marriage always has three levels – physical, emotional and intellectual; and for some people there is a fourth – spiritual. When we promise in the marriage service to love our spouse, to be faithful, and to 'cleave' to him or her alone, we do not specify that only the physical side is meant. We should be aware, therefore, that for one partner to seek satisfaction and 'togetherness' from a third party on any of the four levels can be very damaging to the marriage relationship.

A hard doctrine

Some Christians to whom I have talked about what I call 'intellectual (or emotional or spiritual) adultery' have been unable to recognise it as a potential problem in their own or anyone else's marriage. In general these have been men, and sadly it does seem that men tend to be less aware than their wives that things are going wrong on – say – an emotional level until it is too late. If people regarded these other kinds of 'adultery' as being just as significant as the physical kind, they might give their partners less desire to commit that sin.

Some people accept the general principle but object to the use of the word adultery to describe it, so I shall call it 'infidelity'. It would be wrong, however, to assume that this lessens the seriousness of the situation, for other kinds of infidelity can sometimes be more hurtful to the injured partner than the physical kind.

What I mean by this non-physical infidelity is the situation where a husband or wife does not have the rapport with their partner which they feel they need and therefore goes to someone else, just as many do for sexual satisfaction. A woman (or a man) may have deep emotional needs which her down-to-earth husband finds it difficult to relate to; she will obviously need someone to whom she can open her soul, and if this tends to be the same person all the time, a situation of infidelity can arise. Similarly, a man (or a woman) may want to talk to someone on a deep intellectual level for which he feels his wife could be inadequate, or he may have left her behind spiritually and may prefer to talk and pray with others instead.

There are two obvious differences between these relationships with a third party, and the kind where sexual activities are involved. The first is that even one act of intercourse constitutes physical adultery, whereas it is not necessarily true to say that intellectual infidelity has occurred just because there has been one deep conversation. It should be possible to recognise the danger at an early stage, confess it to your partner, and take steps to avoid it getting worse. The second difference is that for normal people an extra-marital sexual affair will occur with someone of the opposite sex, whereas in the other three areas the relationship could equally be with someone of the same sex. Whether this poses as great a threat will be considered later.

These different kinds of infidelity hurt most when they affect the area of your marriage which you felt was best. For a time our sex life was not very good, mainly due to my reluctance, and I felt that if my husband were tempted to have an affair (though I trusted him not to) it would be partly my fault. On the other hand, our intellectual relationship had always been excellent, and even before we were going out together regularly we were closer on that level than many married people are. If I had found out that he had started having such deep conversations with another woman, I would have felt more hurt than if he had been to bed with her, because intellectually I really felt I had given him everything.

Other writers' views

It's interesting that, although this phenomenon is very little talked about and is rejected as exaggerated by some Christians, several writers actually accept it as a fact. In James Dobson's *Love Must be Tough* one of the women he interviewed, whose husband was very promiscuous, said that the one affair he had which was only emotional and not physically sexual was very painful to her. She felt 'a greater sense of disloyalty' when she pictured her husband sharing himself with another woman than if he had been sleeping with her. This may have been because she was already resigned to his wayward sexual habits but felt that on the emotional side their marriage still had something going for it.

In *We Believe in Marriage* Eileen Mitson comments on a case in which a woman could not share her deep feelings with her husband, though he was kind and clean-living. She had found another man with whom she could communicate emotionally, and though she had no intention of breaking up her marriage she believed that one day she would be free to marry her new friend. Eileen Mitson felt that this emotional infidelity was lulling the woman's conscience and impairing her judgement, regardless of whether or not it led to physical adultery. Some see the emotional relationship as threatening because if it combines with a sexual affair, it is more likely to become a marriage-breaker than if it is based simply on physical attraction. I maintain, however, that infidelity in any area can be a threat, if not to the continuation of the marriage, then at least to happiness within it.

Among secular writers also there can be a feeling that an act of non-physical infidelity can be damaging to a relationship. In the film *Alfie* the hero, who regards his sexual prowess and conquests as all-important, is jealous of his girl-friend's friendship with another man. When she points out that there is nothing sexual in it and they just enjoy talking, Alfie retorts that it is their 'innocent talk' that he objects to because it is 'more intimate than the other'. He recognises that if she has found a man to whom she can communicate her deep thoughts and feelings, she is more likely to establish a lasting relationship with him than with one who can only offer her sex.

An article published in *She* magazine, in 1985, entitled *Can You Be Unfaithful With Your Clothes On?* was discussed by its author Andrea Newman on *Woman's Hour* with the Christian writer Margaret Cundiff. I could not agree with Ms Newman, any more than Margaret Cundiff did, since she was suggesting that extra-marital sex can in some circumstances be harmless; but I certainly agreed with her premise that other non-physical acts could indicate unfaithfulness to one's partner. Examples she gave were character assassination, keeping secrets from your partner, and telling him that you love your children more than you love him.

Physical
To emphasise the seriousness of other kinds of infidelity does not in any way lessen the gravity of physical adultery. According to James Dobson in *Love Must Be Tough*, an appallingly large number of people commit adultery while retaining positions of responsibility in the church, and in some cases even claim that God has sanctioned the new relationship. The Bible states so frequently that adultery is wrong (starting with the commandment in Exodus 20.14) that these people are obviously deluding themselves. Anyone who has the problem of a partner who is having an

affair cannot do better than read *Love Must Be Tough* and consider putting its radical advice into effect. Similarly, anyone who has had an affair and wants to return home and be forgiven will find good counsel in Selwyn Hughes's *Marriage As God Intended*.

Dr Dobson points out that many victims of adultery tend to blame themselves in order to excuse their partner's conduct, thus losing their self-esteem and forfeiting any respect their partner may have retained for them. He claims that no amount of frigidity or other inadequacy is an excuse for a spouse to commit adultery – though this does not mean that we should feel free to act capriciously and be unmindful of our partner's sexual needs. It is of paramount importance that we try to please our partner sexually, that we accede to any reasonable requests, and do not give him or her any reason to *want* to commit adultery. This is the salient point, for some people will be promiscuous, even if they have an attractive and available partner at home, simply because that is their nature and they have not allowed God to change it. On the other hand, some will resist the temptation of an extramarital affair even if they get no satisfaction within marriage. Our conscience should be more concerned with whether we have made our partner want to commit adultery, than whether or not he has actually done so.

Jesus' teaching carries adultery one stage further back than intercourse. He says, 'Anyone who looks at a woman lustfully has already committed adultery with her in his heart' (Matthew 5.28). This can be applied to men who gain sexual stimulation from looking at 'girlie' magazines, and if I found that my husband needed to do that I would feel that something was seriously wrong with our sex life. I am often amazed by the number of women who feel it is natural for their men to want to look at pictures of other women; a Christian man should recognise how easily he is turned on by sight, and therefore make sure he keeps to looking at the woman he has married (and she, of course, should allow him to).

Another situation which could be regarded as committing

adultery in your heart is simply being attracted to someone. A line has to be drawn between acknowledging that a person of the opposite sex is attractive and *could* appeal to you, and deciding that they appeal so much that you want them. Many couples with a mature and stable relationship are able to discuss this and tell each other which of their friends they could fancy; they can often laugh about it together and may be surprised at the things that have attracted their partner. This is a healthy thing to do because it brings any feelings out into the open where they will probably evaporate. Nothing is more likely to grow into a dangerous desire than an emotion that is subdued and not acknowledged.

Intellectual
Stuart and Janice had a very close friendship with another couple, perhaps mainly on the intellectual level, but including spiritual and emotional aspects as well. Because they met together as a foursome, they were all able to relate well without any jealousy arising or any deep subjects being shared which excluded the others. After a while, however, Janice realised that she was too attracted to Adrian, and that the relationship could pose a threat to her marriage. Fortunately she was able to share this with Stuart, and after they had talked about it and started to spend a bit less time with Adrian and Kate, the problem disappeared. If she had kept it to herself it could have escalated into something more serious.

Some people confuse the idea of relating on an intellectual level with relating on the same intellectual subject, and assume that a couple will have no problems provided that they are both librarians, for instance, or computer programmers, or psychiatric nurses. This is one form of communication, but it would be far too restrictive to expect to marry someone with whom one could share all the details of one's daily work. A married couple must realise that they may both need other people to whom they can relate on this level, but it is important to ensure that it is not always the same person, specially if that person is of the opposite sex, and that a lot of time is not spent alone together.

It is said that opposites attract, and many people marry partners who work in a very different sort of field. When this happens, try to take some interest in your partner's job – the joys and frustrations of a day at work can be shared even with someone who doesn't understand much about it. The essence of intellectual communication is the ability to talk about important daily issues, to analyse and discuss television programmes, books or plays, and to listen while the other 'sets the world to rights'. Obviously if your partner has a hobby, the more interest you can take in it, the less likelihood there is of trouble developing. If the hobby is one like music, which might need to be discussed in depth with an equally skilled musician, the same safeguards would need to apply as with colleagues from work.

In some circumstances a husband or wife may even feel displaced if their partner has a confidant of the same sex, but this is likely to pose fewer problems. Anna was an intelligent young woman whose husband Nigel had a mind that worked on an even higher level, and who was frequently assailed by intellectual problems which he needed to think through and talk out. He would always share these in the first instance with Anna, but if he still found no peace of mind he would go to visit his friend Gareth and sit talking late into the night. Anna appreciated the fact that he always talked to her first, and as she recognised her limitations she was pleased that he could use Gareth as a sounding-board. If it had been a female friend to whom Nigel went in the middle of the night, Anna might have felt different!

Emotional
An emotional relationship is also something which can arise with someone of the same sex, and to some extent this is inevitable and perfectly harmless. There are bound to be matters which women prefer to discuss with other women, and most husbands would no doubt admit that there are areas of a woman's mind which they simply cannot fathom!

112

The situation can, however, cause problems between husband and wife if you feel that your partner is going to someone else with an emotional need which you would have been able to meet. Laura was a young married woman with a number of emotional problems, and she had a close female friend with whom she found it easy to talk and who seemed to understand and sympathise. Laura went so frequently to this friend for emotional support that, although there could be no question of any physical relationship, her husband began to feel jealous and to think that she was sharing with her friend a part of her that was rightfully his.

Perhaps Laura's husband was really afraid that she was talking about him and sharing her dissatisfaction with her marriage. There is a sense in which it is helpful to do this. If we never talk about our marital problems with anyone else, we miss out on discovering that our friends have similar difficulties. It can be a great comfort and also a help if they have lived through them and can offer constructive advice. If, however, we flaunt our problems to whoever will listen, and take trouble to paint our partner in the blackest possible colours, then we are being disloyal.

In some cases it is good to talk to other people as a couple, but if this is not appropriate we can avoid deceit or disloyalty be relaying the gist of the conversation to our partner afterwards. For example, a wife might say, 'I was talking to Mary this afternoon about how resentful I am of your commitment to your job, and how it keeps causing trouble between us. I discovered that she and Bob went through something similar a few years ago, and she helped me to look at it in a different light.' An interesting guideline for avoiding disloyalty is: never discuss a marriage problem with a friend unless you have already talked about it with your partner.

If emotional problems, especially to do with marriage, are shared with a friend of the opposite sex, this can be very dangerous and can lead to the 'My wife doesn't understand me' syndrome. Even if no physical relationship ever results,

113

it is still very hurtful for the husband (and again it applies the other way round) to know that his wife has been opening up her heart to someone else, not because she needs to indulge in 'girl-talk' with a female friend, but because she relates better to another man than to him.

In some cases a man – and it is more likely to be a man because women seem more aware of these things – may not realise that he is becoming involved in a relationship of this kind until his jealous wife points it out to him. Richard was an elder of the church who had been very supportive to Jacky, a woman of about his age who had gone through a critical time when her husband was very ill. After the crisis had passed, however, Richard's wife Liz noticed that Jacky kept phoning up about the church Youth Club which all three of them were involved in. She never wanted to speak to Liz, and when Richard answered she would talk for ages on a very deep level. Richard found it hard to see that Jacky was leaning too heavily on him and was establishing an emotional rapport which was inappropriate with someone else's husband, but when he saw how much Liz felt hurt and left out, he realised that he must discourage the relationship.

This case illustrates how damaging the non-physical kind of infidelity can be. Even though apparently harmless, it destroys trust for the future and creates suspicion of other relationships. Liz, who had always trusted Richard implicitly as far as the physical side of marriage was concerned, had experienced a shock when she realised that he was in danger of being unfaithful on another level. She was not helped when he accused her of exaggerating and took a long time to acknowledge the situation. This meant that the next time he came into close contact with a woman with emotional needs, Liz was immediately on the lookout for trouble, and Richard felt inhibited in case he unintentionally made the same mistakes again.

Spiritual

When Christians share emotional problems with each other, it nearly always happens that spiritual matters are discussed as well, and it is not easy to draw the line between emotional and spiritual infidelity. The relationship between Richard and Jacky began on a spiritual basis, but because she found him easy to relate to, an over-intense emotional situation arose. Some people feel it is wrong to find fault with any spiritual/emotional relationship among Christians if the intent is innocent. They argue that people like Richard have the valuable gift of befriending, and no curb should be placed on this. But anyone who gives spiritual or emotional support to someone of the opposite sex in a one-to-one situation is in danger of establishing a relationship which could constitute infidelity if one of the parties is married. It is, moreover, easy to avoid. If, for example, a married woman wants to go to an elder of the church with a spiritual problem, the elder can suggest that her husband be present at the counselling session as well. If she feels that this would be too inhibiting, the elder can avoid the dangers of a one-to-one relationship by including his own wife (or a female church worker) in the meetings.

Spiritual infidelity occurs if you find that you are praying and sharing your spiritual thoughts with someone else instead of your partner. This could arise because you have lost the habit of praying together or have problems over it, as described in chapter 7, or because one of you has left the other behind spiritually. More dangerous, however, is the situation in which your partner is not a Christian at all, because he will be quick to find fault if his wife establishes a close relationship with someone else, even if the purpose is for prayer and nothing else. The Christian partner will have to be very careful to attend 'religious' meetings only at times which don't affect family activities, and to make sure that fellowship is always with a group of people and not in ones and twos.

Gail, whose husband Kevin was not a Christian, had a job as a legal executive and was delighted when a Christian solicitor, Barry, came to work in the office. Barry's wife Jane was also a Christian, but she lacked her husband's enthusiasm and degree of commitment. She was a little put out when she went to church with Barry and found that Gail always joined them. For Kevin the situation was even worse, because he could see that Barry was able to relate to Gail spiritually – something that he hadn't even realised she needed – as well as being on the same wavelength intellectually. If all four people concerned had been committed Christians, Gail and Barry's relationship at work would have posed little danger, for then they would have related within the church as a foursome instead of one man and one woman becoming dangerously close to the exclusion of the other two.

Best friends

Another criticism which could be levelled at this theory of different kinds of adultery is that it is unreasonable to expect a man and a woman to be everything to each other, and to be the ideal partner not only physically, but also intellectually, spiritually and emotionally. Personally, I do not think it is unreasonable. As Christians we stand against the worldly view that a man needs a sexual relationship with more than one woman and that it is natural for him to have a mistress; so why should we not expect our marriage partner to be our main support in other areas of life as well? I say 'main' support because obviously we need friends, colleagues and prayer partners, otherwise our life as a couple would be very insular, but if we cannot relate in one or more of the four areas, then perhaps we should not be getting married.

Marriage is a very difficult state in which to live, even with someone for whom you can be 'all in all'. None of us is forced to get married and it seems extreme folly to do so without examining how many of our needs our prospective partner can fulfil. We are apt to be shocked at the fact that the current high divorce figures include quite a lot of marriages among Christians, and I wonder whether that is because Christians actually take less thought about the suitability of their partner than responsible non-Christians do? We are taught – quite rightly – that we should not be 'unequally yoked', and should choose a partner who shares our faith, but this can lead to a tendency to feel that as soon as we find a committed Christian with whom we feel mutual physical attraction we have all we need for a successful marriage. Whether we have common interests and tastes, the ability to communicate, and a good relationship intellectually and emotionally, are perhaps less likely to be taken into account: we feel that the spiritual togetherness is there, so the rest must surely fall into place.

Debbie was in her early twenties when an ex-boyfriend re-entered her life, having become a Christian. Because they now had their faith in common, the young man – and everyone who knew them – assumed that they would get together again, and Debbie went along with this even to the point of nearly getting engaged, until suddenly she realised that she was making a mistake. The shared faith, coupled with the natural attraction for each other, were not enough to be a basis for marriage and certainly not enough to prove that this was the match that God intended. After she had broken off the relationship, her friends at church admitted that they had not been happy about it, although at the time they had appeared to support her. It is very difficult to know what to do if we see a couple heading for what we believe would be a disastrous marriage, but at least we can encourage any young people we are in contact with to consider all aspects of the relationship very carefully.

I heard of a vicar who, when interviewing candidates for marriage, would always ask each of them who their best friend was. When, as usually happened, the girl would name one of the bridesmaids and her fiancé the chap he had chosen for best man, the vicar always replied that in that case they shouldn't be getting married, because in order for their marriage to succeed they should regard each other as 'best friend'. This is excellent advice because it covers far more than the idea of physical attraction or spiritual compatibility; it implies that the marriage partner is the person with whom we want to spend our time because we have many things in common and can really communicate. I am sure that my own marriage has survived through several dreadfully low patches mainly because John and I were very close friends before we ever became lovers.

If you are able to continue to be best friends to each other, you are unlikely to experience the sort of unhappiness which is caused by any of these kinds of infidelity.

Questions to ask

Do you have an extra-marital relationship on any level which is likely to cause your partner concern?

How can you allow your partner to be your best friend and to supply your needs? If there are areas where this does not happen, what changes can you make?

Do you automatically share your thoughts with your partner before telling anyone else?

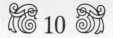

10

'Oh, What Happened to You? . . .'

'. . . Whatever happened to me? What became of the people we used to be?' This theme song of a successful comedy programme contains a great deal of pathos. The words may even point to the main cause of breakdown in some marriages.

Whatever happened to that starry-eyed young couple who were so much in love that they went everywhere with arms round each other and couldn't wait to be alone together? Marriage gave them the sexual freedom they longed for, but now they hardly ever kiss, and they make love only once a fortnight.

And then there was another couple – they met at college and used to share their most intimate thoughts, often talking until the small hours and setting the world to rights. The deepest discussion they have now is about where to go for their holidays, and they are always asleep by eleven o'clock.

There was once a young man who used to play squash and go running every morning. Now he is so unfit that he gets out of breath playing football with his four-year-old son. And do you remember the one who was going to live and work with drug addicts in the inner city? Somehow he has turned into an affluent company director with a house in the country.

What about that attractive girl with shining hair and impeccable dress-sense, who made all her own clothes? Marriage and motherhood have made her afraid to look in the mirror, and she hasn't touched the sewing machine for years. There was another girl who was doing research on the world food crisis and always lobbying her MP. Now if she passes Westminster it's en route for a shopping spree or a gourmet dinner.

What happened to the couple who were going to have at least four children and then found that one drove them mad; or the ones who were going to keep open house for the young people in their church but now don't even know them by name; or the ones who felt called to be missionaries but didn't ever get round to applying? Worse still, what about the young man and girl who used to pray together every time they met – until they got married?

Do any of these examples ring a bell with you? Is one of those young men or women the person you married? Is one of them *you?* Have you, as a couple, lost your dreams or togetherness?

Drifting apart spiritually is probably the most serious change that a Christian couple may have to cope with, and a deteriorating sexual relationship can be nearly as damaging. For that reason the subjects have already been dealt with in separate chapters. However, gradual, insidious changes in other aspects of our lives can lead at last to the awful realisation and recrimination: 'You're not the person I married!'

A different person?

A very large number of people get married in what is likely to be the first third of their lives, so it is hardly surprising that they will have a great deal of changing and maturing to do. Teenage marriages are notorious for not lasting. This is because the partners haven't finished growing into the people they are intended to be, and they could end up disappointing each other.

It is possible, of course, that due to extreme circumstances like mental illness, complete turning away from the Christian faith, or the emergence of a previously concealed evil habit, a husband or wife may actually become a profoundly different person from the one who made the marriage vows. In such cases the other partner may feel that they have been fundamentally deceived, and that they should have the right to end the marriage or at least be legally separated. People in this position obviously need to seek expert help and advice for themselves, and, if possible, for their spouse.

In the vast majority of cases, however, it is not justifiable to claim that your partner is no longer the person you married, although it is too easy to get so depressed about your relationship that you begin to think this way. It is understandable that you should feel disturbed when you suddenly realise how much your partner has changed, yet if you look more closely you will see that the change has been a gradual progression, not a sudden metamorphosis. If you examine the marriage year by year, you will see that he stopped playing football because he couldn't fit in the training sessions when he was working late, and she stopped doing cordon bleu cookery when she had to feed the baby every couple of hours. The desire to hang on to his job in a time of high unemployment prevented that trip round the world, and lack of encouragement dampened their enthusiasm for Christian outreach.

Letting yourself go

The picture of the sullen and slovenly middle-aged man and his fat wife with nagging tongue and hair in rollers is one which the cartoonists delight to exaggerate. The changes in our physical appearance may be of minor importance compared with changes in our character, but it is still a good thing to resist a change for the worse.

Of course, our choice in styles of dress will alter to suit our years and our lifestyle; many people may be forced by their work to adopt a more formal or a more casual mode of dress than they would have liked. That doesn't mean, however, that we need to change our basic attitude to how we look. If we used to take trouble over clothes, personal hygiene and general fitness in order to attract our partner when courting, surely we owe it to them even more to keep it up after we are married. Certainly we should avoid any change of attitude which results in not caring what we look like.

It may be reasonable to suppose that the current trend towards fitness and healthy eating will solve the problem of attractive young bodies going to seed, but there are perhaps aspects of this new emphasis that one needs to beware of. Not for nothing has it been described as 'the new religion', and you should be careful about taking it too seriously if your partner does not share your enthusiasm. If you have been accustomed to enjoying 'normal' meals together, it would be difficult for your partner to adapt to the change if you suddenly decided to eat only health foods or to become a vegetarian. Keeping fit through sport is a very good thing, but it could be detrimental to a marriage if you took on a time-consuming course of training which your partner couldn't join in.

There is no need to get neurotic about the fact that you have put on a few pounds in weight or have some grey hairs, even if your partner has managed to avoid these problems. The important thing – besides thinking and acting young – is to make the best of the body God has given you and the resources at your disposal. You can attempt to look like someone your other half will be proud to be seen with. It is sometimes worth dressing to please your partner rather than yourself. A man who has to wear a suit to work may always prefer to dress casually in the evening, but if he doesn't bother to dress up when he takes his wife out, she may resent the fact that he does so for his job but not for her. A woman might prefer going out in an elegant skirt and high-heeled shoes, but if she knows her husband wants to go for a walk across country rather than round the block, she should modify her dress so that she can join in.

Those who have read Marabel Morgan's *The Total Woman* will find innumerable suggestions for outrageously sexy outfits that a wife can wear to greet her husband on his return from work every evening. This presupposes that the wife isn't also rushing in from work, and that she doesn't have to spend that time of day bathing babies or ferrying children to and from ballet or football practice! However, the basic idea is a good one, and you may sometimes be able to have a candlelit dinner at home together, each dressing – or undressing – to please the other.

'Your old men will dream dreams, your young men will see visions'
This quotation from Joel 2:28 is of course a biblical prophecy which tells us how God will speak to people in the last days, but I wonder whether it gives us a hint as to the way we regard ideas as our age increases. Is the young person's vision of the work he feels God has for him or the impact he wants to make on the world destined to become in later years a hazy dream of what might have been?

That is to some extent inevitable. A young couple who are in love with each other and with the Lord will have ideas of wonderful things they can do together to serve him, perhaps on the mission field, perhaps working with disabled people or in a community. In many cases these 'visions' which are perhaps no more than dreams in the first place, arise simply from awareness of needs in the world and the desire to be used by God, with no real understanding of the qualities needed for the job or the plan God has. When Graham and Maria were students they were involved with a home for ex-prisoners and imagined that this might be the work God had for them when they married. However, they soon realised that they didn't have the necessary qualities, and felt they shouldn't pursue this. Certainly people are needed in that sort of work, and there are no doubt many Christians who are sitting comfortably in Bournemouth when they should be serving God in Borneo, but that doesn't mean that anyone who has ever considered missionary work or any other Christian service is the right one to do it.

If you want to discover whether your vision is really from God you should pray together for guidance and ask God to make it equally clear to both of you whether you should proceed with it, and if so, when. Be willing to accept the fact that if you are required to do the work, God will give you the necessary strength, but he might not want you to do it at all. This is relatively easy when considering a specific course of action at a particular time, as John and I discovered when God gave us clear guidance not to apply for a job in India with a missionary society. What is more difficult to deal with is the less tangible feeling that 'Perhaps we ought to do . . . some day. . . .'

Probably the best test of such dreams is time. If they are mere fancies they will fade away, but if they are visions from the Lord they will stay with you even if it takes years for them to be fulfilled. In 1977 we believed that God was telling us to set up a shop in our local town selling Christian books and third world crafts, and we felt quite disillusioned when the plans fell through. For some time we looked for openings in another sphere of service, but the bookshop idea never really went away, and in 1984 God clearly showed us that this was the time to do it. If you share your dream when it first comes, pray about it together and agree that it is a vision, you will be able to keep it alive by talking about it, and this should draw you closer together and be a help to your marriage.

If your vision turns out to be nothing more than a fancy, the important thing is not to let the loss of it turn you into a different person. God may not want you to set up a Christian home for mentally handicapped people, but perhaps he wants you to visit them or pray for those who are working with them. He may not ask you to do famine relief work in Africa, but he could want you to send a large part of your salary there. If a husband and wife continue to share an interest in the things that were once closest to their hearts they will be the same people growing together in a slightly different direction.

Equally, you may have had a totally secular dream or ambition, like setting up a travel company or running a riding stable. This may not turn out to be the Lord's will for you, but there is no need to lose your ability to imagine crazy schemes. When they married, Jim and Mandy intended to travel round the world, but they allowed steady jobs and a

mortgage to deter them: Jim remarked rather ruefully that
as they got older they were increasing the safety margin in
life and becoming less likely to do anything adventurous.
However, they still dream and make plans together, though
on a smaller scale. They believe that if they could fulfil one
of these they would be more likely to go on to something
more ambitious.

In contrast, there is the person who starts married life in
a relatively mundane job with no great visions or ambitions,
and then feels called by God to do something completely
different. As one vicar's wife remarked somewhat plain-
tively, 'I married an electrician!'. She had quite a bit of
adapting to do when her husband's new job cast her in a
new role as well. Here again, the couple will need to be
very much together as they make plans for the future. To
harbour a belief that God wants a great change in your life
without sharing your vision with your partner will lead only
to trouble. Michele Guinness, in *Child of the Covenant*,
describes her initial feelings of horror when her husband
decided that he had been called to the ministry in a Christian
denomination that was unfamiliar to her. She knew it would
so alter her life that it was essential that she should come to
share his vision.

Confronting change
You have to decide whether to accept change as inevitable
or to fight it every inch of the way. If you choose the latter
course, you must confront the changes one by one as they
begin, and not expect to make a clean sweep every decade!
When you examine individual changes you realise that some
should be resisted at all costs, some must be accepted, and
the majority can be entered into together.

Often it isn't easy to see that you are changing, and this
is where good communication can play an important role.
The couple who can communicate will say to each other,
'You've changed since you got that promotion. You're so
withdrawn; aren't you happy at work any more?' Or, 'You
never used to lose your temper about things like that. Why

does it upset you so much now?' Or they might remind each other, 'Didn't we say we'd never spend every evening in front of the television? Now look at us!' This should lead into a sharing of worries and problems, or a profitable discussion on the kind of life you are leading.

Not all changes are bad, of course, and it's very important to be positive and look for any improvements in your partner's behaviour or your relationship. If you have been communicating your problems and dissatisfactions beforehand, then it will be very helpful and encouraging to comment on anything that pleases you, however small it may be; this is particularly so if your marriage is going through a bad patch. However, you have to be more careful if you have not been communicating beforehand. Imagine the effect of saying, 'I'm so pleased that you're beginning to keep the house tidier,' or 'You have changed recently – you've been so polite to my mother,' if you hadn't told your partner what you were unhappy about in the first place!

If you change jobs you will very probably change as you adapt to your new work: you may become more efficient, more authoritarian, less talkative, and so on. You are bound to change as you adapt to parenthood and acquire the skills needed for understanding and managing children; obviously this will lead to fewer problems if you are both involved with the children and so are both changing together. A death or illness in the family may cause someone to change as they cope with grief and take on new responsibilities.

New ideas, new groups of people, a new church, new teaching and ways of worship all tend to influence us. Even a change which is indisputably for the better, like becoming a Christian, can cause problems if it brings with it a very sudden change in lifestyle, and one partner may easily feel excluded. Carol had a problem when her husband (who had not long come to share her faith) became very involved in a Christian drama group which was full of spiritually alive people. Although Carol felt left out at first, she decided to get involved in the group's activities herself, as far as her family commitments would allow, instead of drawing further away. Certainly if the situation cannot be rectified as easily as Carol's could, it must be brought into the open and talked about before the drifting apart increases.

The person God wants

Although it is good if your partner can comment on changes they see in you, it is even better if from time to time you yourself can evaluate what is happening within you. I am wary of the current emphasis in some parts of the church on self-love, as I feel that this can encourage complacency and a tendency to like, as well as love, yourself, regardless of whether you are becoming more like the person God wants. Certainly it does no harm to take stock of yourself and make a note of any changes in your spiritual life, contact with other people, use of money, and way of living. Then ask, 'Am I pleased with this change in myself? Do I believe my spouse is pleased with it? Do I believe God is pleased with it?'

If you and your partner are both Christians, your answers to all three questions *should* be the same, and you should know whether to encourage or resist the change. However, if the three answers are not the same, you can assume that God is right! It is then necessary to discover why you and your partner are out of tune with him, or why you are out of tune with each other and only one is in tune with God.

For instance, a man may be very pleased that his new job is bringing in more money and that he can afford to buy new gadgets for the home and to take his wife out a lot more. She may be pleased with the change as well, but God may show them that they are becoming too materialistic. If they want to change in accordance with God's will they will have to ask what attitude he wants them to have towards their new-found wealth. Or a woman may feel she has made a good change when she becomes more aware of the needs of the elderly in her parish and starts visiting them a great deal, but her husband may think that she is neglecting her duties at home. They will have to discover together what

God is saying to them about it, and then one will have to adapt accordingly.

Finding out what God wants may sound easy, and in theory it may be easy to search for guidelines in the Bible, but in practice it can be very difficult. It is particularly hard to acknowledge that God may not like the things you are doing or the person you are turning into – especially if your partner also dislikes the changes in you. It may be, too, that you don't find it easy to like the person God wants your partner to be. Perhaps you disagree about decisions concerning the children, or you may feel that he is taking life too seriously or getting too involved with helping other people. Since God has brought you together as a couple, he must want you to change your attitude as well, so that you can still be at one.

Togetherness

The Bible talks about becoming 'one flesh' (Genesis 2.24); obviously this is most perfectly expressed in the sexual act, but it also refers to the 'togetherness' which can be felt in all aspects of marriage, as we saw in the previous chapter. It follows that as we adapt to married life and perhaps parenthood, and change with the passing years, we should be growing together rather than apart.

This process will be greatly helped if we have a good spiritual relationship and pray together about the changes, as suggested above. However, non-Christian couples also manage to grow together, so there must be a non-spiritual side to it as well. It is often said that if you live closely with a person you become like them – some even say that this is the case with owners and their pets! If you are close, adopting each other's mannerisms and patterns of speech will probably happen subconsciously, and so will the tendency to think the same things. If you remark on the fact that your partner has just said what was in your mind it will help you both to know that you are growing closer together. Playing word games which involve guessing and mind-reading can also help you to become mentally in tune with each other.

Many married couples have pet names for each other and perhaps even various words which have evolved between them and which are not intelligible to outsiders. It is good to keep these a secret between husband and wife, not only because they can be an embarrassment to others, but because they heighten the awareness of being a separate entity apart from the rest of the world.

Becoming one flesh doesn't mean having no life other than as a couple; that would be very foolish since one partner is almost bound to be left widowed one day. What it does mean is developing interests that you have in common, seeking to enjoy the same things, and making the most of the circumstances in which your tastes coincide. When people are courting they often put themselves out to take an interest in their partner's hobbies and activities; it is very sad if this ceases once the marriage is established.

So what did happen to you and me?
What can we do if we don't become aware of changes for the worse until it is too late to stop them?

First, we must ask our partner what upsets them about the way in which we have changed. This is vitally important because it shows that we care about what they think and it may help to reopen lines of communication which are becoming disused. If it is hard for you to speak about your feelings, or you find a discussion usually becomes an argument, you may prefer to write down your thoughts and share them on paper before starting to talk about them. It is sometimes helpful if you both make a list of the things you like and the things you dislike about each other. It is important to be positive and to begin the discussion from a point of agreement.

It could be that you just don't like the person your partner has become over the years. Ask yourself why they are like this. You may find that what has grown into a fault was one of the things which attracted you in the first place. Yvonne felt that her husband was over-serious, but she admitted that his sense of responsibility had impressed her when they were courting. Or the change may be due to a decision you have made together, for example regarding work or children. Matthew found his wife to be far more on edge and harder to live with than when they were first married, but he realised that this was due to the strain of having three children close together.

If the problem arises from 'letting yourself go', then obviously drastic measures may be needed in the realms of diet and exercise, or a visit to the hairdresser or tailor! However, there is no point in embarking on this without first assessing why you or your partner have reached this state. Perhaps you are afraid that you can't afford the time or money to spend on your appearance, or you may feel that your partner doesn't care about you any more so there is no point in bothering.

Although some youthful dreams are bound to fade with time, problems will come if one of you retains the dream and one doesn't, or if relinquishing it has turned you into a less interesting and exciting person. In the former case the best thing is obviously to discuss it and pray about it. You may have to face the fact that you should have carried out your dream but now it is too late. You will have to ask forgiveness and then put it behind you and look to the future together. The other possibility may be less serious but harder to rectify: if you have degenerated into a boring person with no original ideas, your partner may be drawn to people who have more energy and zest for living. Isn't it worth making an effort to change, for that reason alone? It may help to have a reminiscenses session together, looking at photos of things you used to do and discussing how you feel about them now, or better still, make an effort to go out and do more things together.

Whatever the reason for the change, it is easy to feel cheated if your partner is very different from the person you expected him or her to grow into. There is no simple answer, but it helps to talk about it and look honestly at how much you have changed as well. If both of you are concerned about what is happening to you and whether you can do anything about it, you are probably halfway to a solution. If, however, only one of you seems concerned, or if communication is so bad that the very idea of talking it through is out of the question, then you may feel that you have reached breaking point.

Questions to ask

In what ways – if any – have you changed into a less exciting, less spiritual or less attractive person than the one your partner married?

In what way have you contributed to some of the adverse changes in your partner?

Do you *want* to become more like the people you used to be?

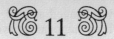

11

Don't Give Up!

In many marriages the problems may be far greater than those described in the last chapter. Alternatively, a combination of small problems will have led to an intolerable situation. Judging from the broken marriage statistics, most people would assume that the next step after this is the divorce court. But is there another alternative?

Some Christians, of course, are divorced against their will and under the present law, if your partner has lived away from you for two years, you can do nothing to prevent it. Others, whose partner may have developed serious problems resulting in cruelty, homosexuality or drug abuse, may find after seeking help that separation (with or without divorce) is the only course open to them. Someone whose partner is beginning to indulge in adultery or other unreasonable behaviour should – as I suggested earlier – try to adopt James Dobson's principles of loving toughness and hope to nip the problem in the bud.

Since whole books are written on the subject of these serious problems alone, I am not attempting to deal with them here. I am writing this chapter for those Christians who for various reasons have realised that their marriage is simply not satisfactory to themselves, not helpful to their partner or their children and consequently not honouring to God – and who are therefore strongly tempted to give up.

Emptiness

When the divorce law was being reformed in the late sixties, one report suggested that when the marriage had irretrievably broken down, the empty legal shell should be destroyed as painlessly as possible. In the version I read there was an unfortunate misprint, and the report contained the words 'empty legal *hell*'! These words describe exactly what marriage has become for some people. As Christians we think of hell as a place of suffering and separation from God; add to that Sartre's well-known phrase, 'Hell is other people', and you have summed up an unhappy marriage – suffering because you are tied to another person, and feeling separated from God because of your failure.

What has happened to the love which sparked off the relationship in the first place? It may be that both partners admit to having lost their love for each other, or perhaps one admits it while the other, though he claims that his (or her) love is as strong as ever, doesn't show it by his actions. In *We Believe in Marriage* Joyce Huggett describes how her husband told the marriage counsellor that he loved his wife and wanted her alongside him but admitted, 'It seems as though Joyce's depression is all my fault but I don't know how to help her.' He was advised that he must show his love for her by allowing her to grow into the person God intended. I found this particularly moving, not only because Mrs Huggett admitted to having such problems, even though she and her husband were well-known counsellors themselves, but also because I could visualise a similar situation in my own marriage.

If you feel you have no love left, should you tell your partner? Since I am always in favour of honesty and openness, I would be inclined to say, do share it. If the love is later restored, you can rejoice in it together, and in the meantime your partner may be more likely to sit up and take note of the fact that you are really unhappy. On the other hand, to say this to a partner who already has a low self image could be disastrous. It should be said very gently without attempting to assassinate every aspect of your partner's character. For example, 'I just can't stand you, I'll never love you again, I don't want to be with you and I can't think why I married you!' could virtually sign the death warrant of a relationship, whereas, 'I know you've done all you can for me over the years, you're a good father to the children and I really respect you, but I just don't seem to love you as a husband any more', is more constructive and gives hope for the future.

Listing our partner's better points is not only good for his morale, but it helps us to see the relationship in perspective. There must have been reasons for choosing that person in the first place, and even if we feel he or she has changed out of recognition, some good points are bound to have remained, and others may have developed over the years. It may be that we are well aware of our partner's many virtues as they appear to outsiders but wonder why the patience, gentleness, generosity and understanding are never directed at us! Probably the hardest thing to take in marriage is the fact that a person who spends his day controlling his emotions and being nice to people then comes home and takes it all out on you, the one he is supposed to love most in the world. If you complain of this treatment you should always consider whether you are guilty of behaving in a similar manner. You could also make an effort to enter into the frustrations of your partner's day instead of immediately feeling hurt and resentful. However, this does not mean that the behaviour should go unchallenged. It is something which needs to be discussed and prayed about, because no married person should have to feel that they are a door-mat to receive the brunt of all their partner's adverse emotions.

Failure to love
You may be aware of your partner's good points and wish you could love him as he deserves but find that you are unable to; so to everything else you add guilt at failing to love such a worthy person. With great honesty Selwyn Hughes, in *Marriage as God Intended*, admits to a time

when his love for his wife had grown cold, and he knew it was largely his fault because he had allowed his work to become more important than his family. He happened to read a detailed description of *agape* love based on 1 Corinthians 13.4–8, and he realised that this was an element that was sadly lacking in his marriage. He asked God to refill his almost empty cup and to enable him to love his wife in the way Paul describes. At the same time he made a deliberate effort to change the direction of his will and to act in a loving way towards his wife. As a result his love for her was rekindled.

God is love, and love comes from him, so there is surely nothing strange about asking him to help us to love someone, especially if it is someone we have already promised to love for a lifetime. God is able not only to restore dying feelings but also to give a new dimension of love to a marriage. His love is able to strengthen whichever aspects of a marriage may be failing, and he is more than ready to restore that indefinable feeling which enables you to tell someone you love them. God does not utter a magic spell which works overnight, but brings about a long slow miracle which works because you believe it will. I tried it in desperation; and after a while God showed us that the love he can give is deeper than the kind we had achieved ourselves.

Communication

The ability to talk together and communicate your real feelings and thoughts is a key factor in all marriages; without it our problems are magnified. Because I rate communication so highly, I have not singled it out as a separate subject, but have tried to mention it in every chapter so that it is seen as an integral part of every aspect of life.

There are many subjects on which communication is essential *before* marriage, such as contraception, the desire to have children, money, attitudes to both partners' work and the emphasis placed on spiritual matters. If, as an engaged couple, you cannot discuss these matters *and come to agreement* on them, then trouble is likely in the future. However, if you did enter into marriage ill-prepared and possibly ill-suited, that doesn't mean that there is no hope for you. Just as we can ask God to give us love for our partner, we can also ask him to help us to communicate and reach agreement on issues where there has been stalemate.

Discussion needs to continue throughout marriage as circumstances force you to change your ideas, or revise your plans. A couple may discuss the direction they expect their careers to take and the area they plan to live in, but then God may lead them otherwise, as we have seen. When you are young and healthy, with good job prospects, it is difficult to have a realistic discussion on how you would deal with illness, long-term unemployment, or senile parents. It is not always possible to gauge how you will view financial priorities until you have a mortgage, insurances and children. It is important, however, to establish at the beginning of a marriage (or, failing that, at whatever stage you have now reached) *lines* of communication in all subjects which can be used whenever necessary.

On the less important subjects, of course, agreement is by no means always necessary: not only would life be rather dull if we had to agree on everything, but it would also be very difficult to find anyone with whom we were compatible enough to marry. The most important thing is the *ability* to communicate, not the fact that you do it indiscriminately. If, after some time of communicating explosively on – say – politics, you decide that you will never agree and only get upset discussing it, then it may be wiser to call a truce and choose not to discuss politics in the normal course of events. This is not failure to communicate, it is victory over your natural desire to argue your point of view and influence your opponent.

The unruffled husband
There are probably three communication problems which can arise in a marriage which is failing: one is the inability to communicate at all – the prolonged silence, the bottled

up resentment, the repressed anger; another is constant bickering and quarrelling; and the third is the situation in which one partner wants to argue about something but the other is impervious to it. Very often it is the women who like to air their grievances and the men who are calm, placid, indifferent and phlegmatic. In this situation, not only does the man refuse to be drawn into an argument with his wife or to defend himself against her taunts, but he also appears to let the rest of the world ride rough-shod over himself and his family. When his wife screams at him, 'Are you a man or a mouse?' he just mutters biblical verses about turning the other cheek. It is disheartening for a woman to feel that she has a husband who won't stand up for her or fight for his rights in the outside world. A further problem is that such men often tend to be too trusting and gullible – then if they are let down, the whole family suffers. It is frustrating for the wife to be almost totally ignored when she gets worked up about something – it's like fighting a sponge – and she begins to feel guilty about complaining when her husband is such an easy-going sort of chap.

Because passive husbands also appear tolerant and good-natured to their friends and relations, the wife will get no sympathy at all unless she can find someone who is suffering in a similar manner. The trouble is that if the man's attitude to life changes, as it may well do with time, things are not usually any better. Eileen used to get frustrated because her husband was so trusting and was often hurt and let down by people, but as he grew older his many experiences made him cynical and pessimistic; she admitted that she preferred the way he used to be. Ron's wife Sue was the highly-strung argumentative type who couldn't stand the way he let everyone – including her – trample on him, but after some years Ron went to the other extreme and had phases of trying to assert himself most forcefully. Sue suddenly found that if she said the wrong thing he might fly into a rage and shout and throw things, and if she happened to mention that any money was owing to them, he was almost tempted to engage in a law-suit. Wives in Sue's situation get even less sympathy than they did before, because usually the Rons of this world don't show their violent side except in the home, and no one is willing to believe that it exists.

This could sound a pretty hopeless state to be in, but all is not lost if you start by asking God to rekindle or increase your love for your partner. Then count your blessings: if you are married to a sponge, be thankful that you needn't be in constant fear that he will hit you, and if you have an assertive husband, rejoice that you can rely on him to stand up for you (and to you!). Thirdly, choose a time when your partner is not tired, hungry, worried, or sexually frustrated, and try to have a friendly discussion on the fact that he (or she) never seems to show emotion or to defend himself (or that he reacts too violently). Invite him to make similar criticisms of you and *listen to them*. Tell him that you need to understand him better and ask him if he could try – for your sake – to put his feelings into words instead of retreating behind a wall of sulking or violence. Above all, try to pray about it together – or – if that is too much at this stage, pray yourself about praying together, and about the problem.

Angry words

In some marriages both partners are equally argumentative, and when they hit a bad patch it seems that they cannot open their mouths without quarrelling. This is not worse than no communication at all, because the opposite of love is not hate but indifference, and the quarrelling couple at least feel strongly about each other, while the sullen, silent ones may be verging on indifference. However, all quarrelling is unpleasant and exhausting, and unsettling for children if you have them, and it may be necessary to place limitations on communication in certain areas in order to calm things down a bit.

In our own marriage, we know that the subject of money is the one which is always most likely to produce a quarrel, yet at one stage we found we were often discussing it late at night when we were tired and therefore more irritable than usual. The more we 'communicated', the more sleep we lost and the more implacable we became, so we made a pact that the subject of money was not to be brought up late in the evening; this was a distinct improvement for us. The lines of communication are there, but we both think twice before using them at the wrong time.

James Dobson, in *Love Must be Tough*, emphasises the need to maintain the line of respect and to tell your partner when you find his or her conduct unacceptable. This is a good principle, but it still needs to be used under God's guidance. It is wise not only to pray about what you say before entering into such a confrontation, but also to ask God to show you the right time (if any) to do it. Communication for the sake of it, without considering the time and place, has no virtue, nor has the determination to pursue an argument to the bitter end, just to have the last word. Sometimes a marriage problem has already been discussed ad nauseam, and nothing further can be gained by 'communicating' and causing another quarrel. In such cases it may be essential to share the problem with an outsider – a professional counsellor, an elder of the church, or a friend who has suffered in a similar way.

A seemingly trivial, but very real, bar to successful communication can be personal appearance: it may sound stupid to suggest that because your husband has a spot on his nose or is wearing his most unbecoming sweater you are more inclined to quarrel, but I have found this is so. Try to take note of whether you find fault more easily with your partner (or your children or friends for that matter) if there is something about their clothes or general appearance which displeases you. I certainly find that I have less patience with my children's faults if they are wearing ill-fitting clothes or have a shirt hanging out (even if it is my fault that the old clothes haven't been replaced!). If you agree that this can happen, you will need to avoid discussing a contentious issue in these circumstances, and you will want to take a look in the mirror and make sure that your own clothes, hair, and face are not going to spark off an adverse reaction.

When things reach the point at which you want to shout

at each other (regardless of how you are dressed!) you will be less free to do so if you have children than if you haven't, because children don't understand the relative insignificance of some adult quarrels, nor do they necessarily understand that their parents would never leave each other, no matter how bad things become. J. Allan Petersen said, 'A child's most basic security is in knowing that his parents love each other. It is even more important than their love for him.' Children nowadays see so many marriages fail that they may tend to watch their parents particularly closely, feeling that their own security is at stake. Diana, now very happy in her second marriage, finds that her children, whose father walked out after many quarrels, now hate any heated discussion between their mother and step-father.

It is often suggested that children would be happier living peacefully with one parent and visiting the other than living in a household of constant bickering and violent quarrels. I have even heard Christians admit that they enjoy being with their children (and with other people) and having pleasant outings and peaceful days at home, so long as their partner isn't around. As soon as he (or she) appears, a friction builds up which rubs off on to everyone else and may cause arguments among the whole family, possibly – though not always – because the children play one parent off against the other. What are these families to do? What is better for the children? My experience is that most children would prefer their parents to stay together in spite of all the quarrels.

Facing up to separation
Christians believe that divorce is wrong: it is obviously bad to break the promises we made before God, the social disadvantages are undeniable, and the Bible makes it clear that divorce should only be the last resort when adultery has ruined a marriage (Matthew 19.8, 9). (I would stress again that I am not attempting to consider cases of child abuse, homosexuality and so on, which I believe fall into a different category altogether.) In Britain, divorce is

140

available for a wider range of circumstances than those mentioned in the Bible, and it has generally come to be seen as the natural result of a bad marriage; even those who disapprove of divorce and wouldn't think of remarrying, have the option of separation. When Christian marriages go wrong, the partners know that these legal options are open to them, and Selwyn Hughes records a large number of couples he has counselled who were contemplating divorce not because of cruelty or adultery, but because life together had simply become an 'empty legal hell'.

Some Christians believe that when we find ourselves living in married hell we should pretend that divorce and separation don't exist, and determine to carry on regardless. I think this is a foolish attitude for several reasons. First of all, if we have reached this state of failure where we are tempted to think of separation, *we have already broken our marriage vows* – we are not loving, cherishing, cleaving – and our marriage is not honouring to God. To pretend that it would be sinful to end the marriage but that in continuing it no sin is committed, is simply self-deception. True, the *effect* on our future lives and our children will be different if we separate, but as far as God is concerned, surely a bad marriage is just as bad as a separation? God can and will forgive the sins we commit, and this applies to the sin of having a bad marriage and wanting to end it just as much as to having a bad marriage and deciding to put up with it.

Secondly, if we are prepared to look separation in the face we may surprise ourselves by finding that we don't really want it after all; whereas if we claim that for us it is not an option it may take on a quite unrealistic glamour. We may honestly feel that life would be more stable for our children if we separated, or we may believe that we could be ourselves more if we weren't tied to our partner. So long as divorce is 'pie in the sky' we can believe these things, but if we face it as a reality we may become aware that nothing would be any better. One couple I heard of had reached the stage of discussing splitting up. The wife pointed out that if she was to have the children she would need to stay in the matrimonial home and her husband would have to leave; he suddenly realised he had nowhere to go other than back to his parents and admitted, 'Whatever I say about you, you're not as bad as my mother!' The marriage has survived!

A Christian couple should surely not discuss or dismiss separation so lightly, but they *may* have to discuss it before they can dismiss it. Cathy and Martin reached a seven-year itch in their marriage and during their frequent quarrels they sometimes threatened to divorce each other; they then repented of their angry words and promised that they would never think of divorce again. When they went through a second, more serious, bad patch some years later, they tried to adhere to this promise but felt only frustration at the thought of being tied to their unhappy marriage for ever. At last they admitted defeat; they knew that although neither had become involved with anyone else they had broken several of their marriage vows and were making a miserable home for their children. It was only when they talked seriously about how a separation could be arranged – where they would live, who would have the children, how they would manage financially – that Cathy particularly was hit by the enormity of it. Suddenly, instead of hurling insults and casual threats of divorce at each other, they were sitting down in cold blood and discussing carving up their home and family, and planning a life of loneliness, hardship and regrets. How would their children cope with seeing their home destroyed? How would their families react? What about the church? Whose 'side' would their friends be on, and would they ever be able to relate to people in the same way again?

The shock of realising what separation would involve did not, of course, solve any of the marriage problems, nor did it stop them feeling for a while longer that the marriage couldn't continue, but it was a turning point. It did enable Cathy to see that ending the marriage wouldn't make her any happier than remaining in it, and Martin began to be more aware of how seriously their problems were affecting

Cathy. In time the Lord healed their relationship and gave them a deep love for each other; having lived through the external problems they emerged with a stronger marriage. They were able to ask forgiveness for the failures in their union which had led them to want to end it, but they did not consider the fact of discussing separation as a specific sin greater than the rest.

Who do we go to for help?
Most people need someone to talk to when their marriage is on the rocks. Confiding in a trusted friend is not the same as slandering your partner around the neighbourhood. It is essential, however, to find the right person, otherwise you might receive unhelpful advice or hurtful indifference. James Dobson quotes many people whose marriages became worse when they followed advice to be a doormat and turn the other cheek. I also believe that it is unhelpful to say in a shocked voice, 'You are a Christian; you shouldn't even think of divorce!'

As Christians we are constantly told to help each other and share our burdens, but it is not easy to do this where marriage problems are concerned. If we do not share them in our Christian fellowship, we may find ourselves going to a church service or meeting in deep misery, too preoccupied with our own problems to participate, and going home feeling no better – or perhaps we stay at home all along because we know how it will be. If we do share the problems (and I mean in a small group, because obviously it would be inappropriate in a large one) we may meet with an embarrassed silence because people just don't know what to say (as in bereavement), or they might try to jolly us out of it and minimise the problems, which is insulting to us and no help at all.

In fact, the people who react in this way may be very concerned (once they are convinced that you are serious), and even if they can't think of anything to say they may be praying quietly for you or trying to help in practical ways. When you need an unshockable person who will listen, it is easy to criticise those who don't have this gift; but in fact people may prove that they care in other practical ways by helping to relieve the situation – looking out for jobs for an unemployed person, for instance, or helping to care for a sick relative. I know from experience that if you pray specifically – say during a church service – for the Lord to lead you to someone to talk to, he will do so, even though it may not be the person you expected, and they may offer to help in a way you hadn't realised you needed.

An unhelpful response is when a counsellor feels there is so much bitterness between a couple that he has to see them separately. This seems odd when we often hear about the importance of both partners going for counselling, but perhaps the best solution would be for both to go separately to the same person rather than being interviewed together. In some cases a couple who suffer from lack of communication may find that the presence of a minister or other trained person helps them to open up on subjects they can't normally talk about. But those whose communication is already unrestrained may become even more bitter in the presence of someone who they had hoped would act as a go-between. They may be the ones who need to be counselled separately.

Sometimes a totally untrained person can actually be more help than a professional if it is someone who was (or still is) in the same situation themselves; provided of course that the two don't start wallowing in their problems together. Such confidants can be invaluable because they are unshockable and uncondemnatory, and they may be able to offer practical advice which they have themselves tried and tested. This is so much more helpful than a pious reaction of, 'Do you pray about it together? No? Well then of course your marriage won't be right if you're not right with the Lord', without any indication of how you and your partner can regain the relationship in which you can even think of praying together.

The major problem about seeking help from this kind of experienced but untrained person is that you simply may not know of anyone who has been in a similar situation to yourself in whom you can confide. If you have suffered a bereavement, or are coping with a handicapped child, you will probably know of others in like circumstances to whom you can relate, but people tend to hush up marriage problems. Also, if help is sought only from those who are themselves experiencing problems or who have the emotional scars of previous ones, then a vicious circle is likely to arise in which the same people are leaned on all the time until they feel unable to manage. The stronger people, who could perhaps cope with several friends crying on their shoulder, are not used in this capacity because they have less to offer. It would certainly be a good thing if all Christians were more sensitive to the needs and problems of those in their fellowship, even if they are tempted to feel that such problems shouldn't exist in the church. If there were more openness about difficult marriages, we all might feel more able to share our problems before becoming submerged by them, and without fear of being made to feel a freak or a failure.

Don't give up!
So if you have reached the point where you feel your marriage has nothing more going for it, or if you despair of being able to talk to anyone about it, my message is: Don't give up! Be prepared to face your problems and discuss them frankly but sensitively with your partner. Don't be afraid to ask for help from other Christians or from professional counsellors. More Christian couples than you realise have been here before you, and with God's help have come through their crises, sometimes to an even stronger and closer relationship.

I have tried to stress throughout this book that every marriage is individual and that there are no set formulae that will work for everyone. However, other people's experiences and suggestions can be useful, so I make no apology for ending with a list of some of the things which helped us to rebuild a failing marriage and which made it seem more worthwhile trying. I sincerely hope that these ideas will be a help to many of you, too.

Factors in rebuilding a failing marriage

Seeing people whose marriage has less going for it than yours and yet who manage to make it work.

Seeing the misery and bitterness that arises when people split up.

Facing the fact that permanent separation is a possibility, and considering whether you would really want to live in that state.

Realising that quarrelling is a waste of your life and that you are probably halfway through it and could die any day.

Seeing your partner suffering from an illness and wondering how you would feel if he or she died.

Encountering people who are being unpleasant about something, so that you can both stand together against them.

Praying to be given love for your partner, just as you might a difficult colleague or neighbour, only more so.

Being positive about your relationship and noting every slight improvement as if it had taken you one rung back up the ladder.

Trying to regard your partner as a friend rather than an enemy, and putting the best interpretation on what he or she does and says.

If you feel cross or miserable about something outside your marriage, explaining to your partner what the problem is and that it's not their fault.

When bouts of happiness do occur, telling each other of your love and appreciation.

Making love when one of you wants to, instead of waiting until you both do.

Trying to have at least a short prayer together last thing every night.

Occasionally trying to do something difficult or distasteful to please your partner, or arranging pleasant surprises.

Bibliography

Chave-Jones, M., *Coping with Depression*. Lion 1981.

Dobson, J., *Love Must Be Tough*. Kingsway 1984.

Elliot, E., *Let Me Be a Woman*. Hodder 1979.

Elliot, E., *The Mark of a Man*. Hodder 1981.

Guinness, M., *Child of the Covenant*. Hodder 1985.

Huggett, J., *Growing into Love*. IVP 1982.

Huggett, J., *We Believe in Marriage*. Marshalls 1982.

Hughes, S., *Marriage as God Intended*. Kingsway 1983.

LaHaye, T. and B., *The Act of Marriage*. Zondervan 1980.

Lawther, G., *Family Planning: The ethics and practicalities of birth control methods*. Triangle/Christian Woman 1985.

Morgan, M., *The Total Woman*. Hodder 1975.

Peck, D., *There's Somebody at the Door*. Triangle 1985.

Stroud, M., *Loving God, Loving You*. Pickering and Inglis 1985.

Sullivan, B., *Your Place in the Family*. Marshalls 1984.

Townsend, A., *Marriage without Pretending*. Scripture Union 1975.

Urquhart, C., *His God, My God*. Hodder 1983.

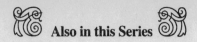

Also in this Series

Family Planning
The ethics and practicalities of
birth control methods

GAIL LAWTHER

This Christian book on contraception
looks at the options available
and is intended for Christians
who are married or planning to marry
and who wish to regulate their fertility
in a way compatible with their faith.

Gail Lawther has researched the subject carefully
and discusses in a Christian light
the methods available, their practicalities, the risks
and the advantages and disadvantages of each.
Special attention is paid to the
ethical questions involved and to the
new problems raised for Christians
by some of the most recent research.
Couples who are concerned to make the right choices
with each other and before God will find her approach
particularly helpful and informative.

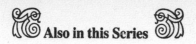

Creativity
Using your talents

EILEEN MITSON AND OTHERS

'In the beginning God created ...'
and we, his children, made in his image,
also have the desire to create.
Creativity is God's gift to us.

If therefore our lives are open to him,
he will show us areas in every aspect of life
in which we can create new growth –
our homes, families and environment,
in our relationships and in our own
personalities and talents.
He has already provided us with the raw materials –
we can use them to build or destroy –
we can choose to be on the side of life, or of death.

Nine women who have chosen life
have contributed to this thought provoking book,
which will inspire every Christian woman
to explore new ideas and to develop
her own unique creative potential.

Also in this Series

Birthright?
A Christian woman looks at abortion

MAUREEN LONG

Like many Christian women,
Maureen Long is deeply concerned about
current permissive attitudes to abortion.
Her book reveals the enormous scale
of the problem, in terms of lives destroyed,
and also other less publicised aspects,
such as the long-term effects on the mother,
and potential family and social problems.
All these are discussed in the light
of the Bible's teaching about
the sacredness of life.

Birthright? calls on Christians
to fight for legal and social recognition
of every child's right to be born,
and gives practical suggestions about how
this can be done, including information
about pro-life societies and
organisations.

**For a complete list of *Christian Woman* titles
see the front of this book**